UNIT C

ENERGY, WORK, AND MACHINES

Theme: Systems

GET READY TO

OBSERVE & QUESTION

What are work and friction?

Are the people in this picture working, or playing? It might surprise you to learn that work is being done as the toboggan races down the hill. But who or what is doing the work? How would this picture be different if it was summer instead of winter?

EXPERIMENT & HYPOTHESIZE

How can energy be changed to other forms?

Studying the behavior of a bouncing ball will help you learn about different kinds of energy and about how energy changes from one kind to another. This activity can also help you learn how energy is stored in different kinds of matter.

INVESTIGATE!

RESEARCH & ANALYZE

As you investigate, find out more from these books.

- *Racing the Iditarod Trail* by Ruth Crisman (Dillon Press, 1993). This book traces the history of a famous sled dog race. It also describes a sport in which a great deal of energy is used to do work.

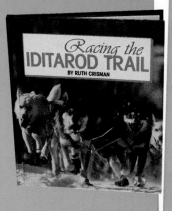

- *The Winter Room* by Gary Paulsen (Dell, 1991). What kinds of tools were used on a Minnesota farm years ago? How are these tools related to simple machines that we use every day? Read this book to find out.

WORK TOGETHER & SHARE IDEAS

How can you model the building of an Egyptian pyramid using simple machines?

Working together, you'll have a chance to apply what you've learned to an ancient project—the building of the pyramids in Egypt. Find out if your group can use energy, work, and machines to overcome some of the obstacles faced by the Egyptians as they were constructing the Great Pyramid at Giza.

CHAPTER 1

ENERGY AND WORK

You're climbing ever so slowly upward. As you look skyward, your heart pounds, and you tightly clutch the safety bar over your lap. You finally reach the top, pause for one agonizing moment, and then hurtle downward with terrifying speed! You're on a roller coaster, a ride that zooms with energy.

Designing for Speed

Ron Toomer is a mechanical engineer who designs roller coasters. President of Arrow Dynamics, Inc., of Clearfield, Utah, Toomer has designed some of the highest roller coasters in the world.

When Ron Toomer begins to design a roller coaster, he builds a model to help him visualize the ride. Then, using a computer, he determines how to construct an exciting, but safe, roller coaster whose cars will have enough energy to speed over the entire track. What gives a roller coaster energy? Find out through the Investigations in this chapter.

Coming Up

◄ One of Ron Toomer's roller coasters

WHAT ARE SOME DIFFERENT FORMS OF ENERGY?

Make a list of all the things in your classroom that contain energy. In this investigation you'll discover what forms of energy these things contain, how energy changes, and how it travels.

Activity

It's a Stretch

Do you know how to store energy? In this activity you'll see how to store and release energy—just by working with a balloon and a rubber band.

Procedure

1. Blow up a balloon and tie its neck so that no air escapes.

2. Hold the balloon firmly out in front of you with your fingertips while your partner pushes the eraser end of a pencil into the balloon. Release the balloon. In your *Science Notebook*, describe what happens to the balloon.

MATERIALS
- goggles
- 2 small balloons
- large rubber band
- pencil
- *Science Notebook*

SAFETY

Wear goggles during this activity. When snapping rubber bands, be sure the bands are directed at the intended target only.

Step 2

3. Place the balloon on a flat surface. Make a fist with your thumb pointed up and place a rubber band over the tip of your thumb.

4. Stretch the rubber band back and aim it at the balloon as shown. **Predict** what will happen if you release the rubber band. Release it and **describe** what happens.

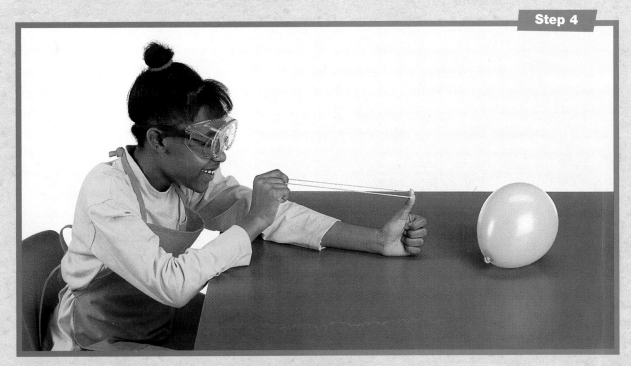

Step 4

5. Blow up a second balloon. Hold the neck tightly, but don't tie it off. **Predict** what will happen if you release the balloon. Release it and **describe** what happens.

Analyze and Conclude

1. How did you store energy in the balloon in step 2? in the rubber band in step 3?

2. Releasing stored energy often causes something to move. In this activity, **tell what evidence** you used to determine that stored energy was released.

3. Moving objects have energy. **Tell what evidence** you observed that indicated that stored energy can be changed to energy of motion.

INVESTIGATE FURTHER!
....

EXPERIMENT

Create your own experiment with a rubber band and a balloon. Be sure to wear your goggles. Describe the energy forms you observe.

Activity
Using Stored Energy

A battery stores energy. In this activity, you can release some of the energy stored in a battery and find out what forms of energy you can get from it.

MATERIALS
- goggles
- AA battery
- 2 pieces of insulated wire with stripped ends
- small bulb
- bulb holder
- electrical tape
- *Science Notebook*

SAFETY /////
Wear goggles during this activity. Don't allow the wire to remain connected to the battery too long. While it is connected, touch only the coated part of the wire.

Procedure

1. Use a small piece of tape to connect one of the stripped ends of a piece of wire to the bottom of a battery.

2. Tape the other bare end of the wire to the small cap on the top of the battery. Carefully feel the wire by holding a section of the coated wire between your fingers. **Record** your observation and then disconnect the wire from the battery.

3. Connect two wires to the bulb holder. Then touch the unconnected ends of the wires to the top and bottom of the battery as shown. **Observe** what happens.

4. Remove the wires from the battery and **record** your observations in your *Science Notebook*.

Step 3

Analyze and Conclude

1. What kind of energy did the battery supply in this activity?

2. What type of energy did you observe in step 2 of the activity?

3. What type of energy did you observe in step 3?

4. Based on this activity, what can you **infer** about various forms of energy?

Energy and Change

As thousands of people roar, an athlete races down a narrow runway. At the end of the runway, she leaps upward and forward. A fraction of a second later, her heels dig into a soft pit. Sand flies in all directions. The roar of the crowd becomes louder as fans in the stands realize that the athlete has broken a world record.

How did the athlete achieve her great feat? For one thing, she used energy to make things happen, or change. As a matter of fact, this is one way to describe energy: **Energy** is the ability to cause change.

Changes Caused by Energy

If you were to watch a replay of the athlete's record-breaking leap, you might discover some of the changes caused by the energy she produced. Look at the picture on this page. What changes do you see?

Energy can cause an object to change position. The athlete used energy in her muscles to move down the runway. That's a change of position.

Energy can make things change speed or direction. The athlete changed speed as she dashed down the runway. She changed her direction when she

What changes are caused by the athlete's energy? ▼

Sound energy can shatter glass (*left*) and damage eardrums (*right*).

jumped into the air.

Energy can also cause temperature to change. If you could have taken the athlete's temperature, you would have found that it went up while she was running and leaping. Energy released in her body made this happen.

Kinds of Energy

There are many kinds of energy, and each kind can cause things to change. The athlete used mechanical energy to make things change. Mechanical energy includes everything having to do with an object's motion.

If you watched the track event on television, you used electricity, another form of energy. In most power plants, coal or oil is burned to produce heat energy, which is used to make electricity. The burning of fuel releases energy that has been stored in the fuel's chemicals for millions of years. This kind of stored energy is called chemical energy.

You have already seen chemical energy being used. In the activity on page C8, the electricity in the wires came from chemical energy that was stored in the battery.

It doesn't have to take millions of years to store energy in something. In fact, you can store energy in this book just by lifting it up and holding it steady. "Come on," you might say, "there's nothing in this book but pages." OK, then let go of the book. What happens? The book moves toward the floor. All of a sudden, it has energy of motion. Where did the book get that energy? You put it there when you picked up the book. And the energy of motion in the falling book is about equal to the energy you used to lift it.

Let's return one last time to the track star. The energy she used in running and jumping came from chemical energy stored in food she had eaten earlier. Now it's time for the woman to "recharge her batteries." With a little rest and a balanced meal or two, she'll be ready to take another shot at the long-jump record. ∎

Energy Transfer

A farmer shades his eyes from the blinding light of a summer day. Waves of heat rise up from the fields around him. Sweat trickles down his tanned neck as he glances at a nearby thermometer. The thermometer reads a sizzling 35°C (95°F).

High in the sky over the farmer's head—150,000,000 km away—is the source of his discomfort. It's the Sun, a blazing star. Deep within the Sun, tremendous amounts of energy are produced continuously. This energy leaves the Sun and travels outward through space in the form of waves. Such energy is called electromagnetic (ē lek'trō-mag net'ik) energy.

Energy Travels in Different Ways

Light is electromagnetic energy you can see. There are other kinds of electromagnetic energy you can't see, such as X-rays, ultraviolet radiation, and infrared radiation.

Electromagnetic energy can travel through empty space. You know this, because energy from the Sun reaches Earth. And there is little between Earth and the Sun except empty space. As stated earlier, electromagnetic energy travels as waves. The transfer of energy by waves is called **radiation**.

If you hold your hand near a hot object—a radiator, for example—you can feel the heat without touching the

Energy from the sun can make you squint and make your skin feel hot. ▼

How does heat travel from the radiator to your hands? ▼

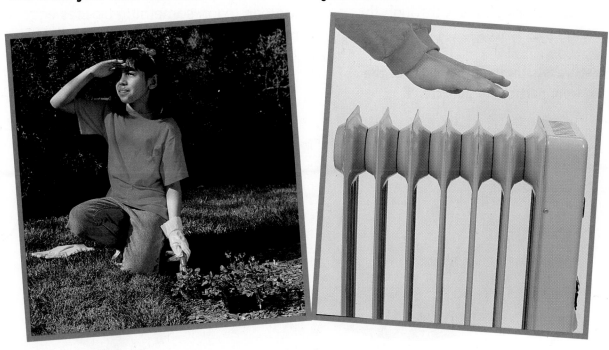

▲ **Why does the last penny move from the row?**

object. Some energy leaves the radiator as infrared radiation. When this invisible form of electromagnetic energy reaches your hand, it is absorbed and changed to heat energy.

All forms of energy can travel from place to place. However, electromagnetic energy is the only form that can travel through empty space. Every other form of energy needs a *medium* of some kind to carry, or transfer, it. A medium may be matter in any of its familiar states—solid, liquid, or gas.

Disturbing Particles

Energy can travel through solid, liquid, and gas mediums by disturbing the particles that make up the mediums. In solids, energy causes the particles to vibrate a bit. But the particles don't go anywhere. They simply transfer energy from one particle to the next. In this way, the energy moves through the mediums as waves.

To get an idea of how this transfer of energy works, lay eight pennies down in a row on a flat surface. Each penny should touch the next penny in line, as shown in the picture. Now take a ninth penny and snap it against a penny at one end of the row. What happens to the eight pennies?

Only the last penny moves. The energy that you gave to the penny you snapped is transferred through the line of pennies to the last penny. The other pennies serve as the medium for the transfer of energy.

Heat and other forms of energy can be transferred through different mediums. Let's say you want to fry eggs in a pan with a metal handle. You place the pan on a hot stove burner. Soon the pan is hot. You drop in butter and eggs, and they begin to sizzle.

If you continue to hold the handle of the pan, soon something besides eggs might begin to sizzle—your hand! This

Heat travels through the metal of the pan from particle to particle. ▼

Warm air rises.

It cools and sinks.

Cool air moves toward the stove.

Cool air pushes up warm air.

▲ **Air in the room is heated by convection.**

happens because heat is transferred through the metal pan to its handle.

Energy is transferred through solids such as the pan by conduction (kən-duk′shən). **Conduction** is the transfer of energy by direct contact between particles. The particles in a solid are packed close together. Energy is simply conducted, or passed along, from one particle to the next.

Energy can also be transferred through fluids—liquids and gases—by the movement of particles. The transfer of heat energy through fluids by moving particles is called **convection** (kən-vek′shən). The picture at the top of this page shows how heat energy from a

stove on one side of a room can warm the air on the other side of the room by convection.

Convection can occur in fluids because the particles in fluids can move about quite freely, carrying heat energy with them. Energy can't be transferred through solids by convection, because the particles remain in fixed positions.

Solids, liquids, and gases can also carry energy as waves. Think about the energy carried by ocean waves, for example. Sound energy travels through air as waves. Unlike electromagnetic waves, however, sound waves can't travel through empty space. Sound travels by "making waves" of air. ■

INVESTIGATION 1

1. Name three kinds of energy and give examples of how each kind can cause a change to occur.

2. Explain why astronauts used radio waves (electromagnetic waves) rather than sound waves to communicate with each other on the Moon.

INVESTIGATION 2

How Can Energy Be Changed to Other Forms?

Where does your body's energy come from? On a sheet of paper, make a drawing of a person. Around the person, draw pictures that show where the person gets energy. Add to your diagram to show where the energy in these sources comes from. Use arrows to show where you think energy changes form.

Activity

To Bounce or Not to Bounce

A flashlight has energy stored in its chemicals. How can an object placed on a high shelf also have stored energy? How can that energy change?

MATERIALS
- small rubber ball
- clay
- meterstick
- *Science Notebook*

SAFETY
Be careful not to lose your balance when standing on a chair.

Procedure

1. Hold a rubber ball in front of you at a height of about 1 m. Release the ball and have your partner **measure** how high the ball bounces. **Record** the height of the bounce in your *Science Notebook*.

2. Stand on a chair and hold the ball at a height of 2 m, as shown. **Predict** how high the ball will bounce after it hits the floor. Release the ball and have a group member **measure** and **record** the height of its bounce.

3. Shape the clay into a ball about the size of the rubber ball. Drop the clay ball from a height of 1 m. **Describe** how the clay looks after hitting the floor.

Step 2

4. Reshape the clay into a ball and drop it from a height of 2 m. **Describe** how the clay looks after it hits the floor.

Analyze and Conclude

1. Tell what evidence you observed that the rubber ball and the clay ball at a height of 1 m had stored energy.

2. What happened to the amount of energy stored in the balls as you raised them from a height of 1 m to a height of 2 m? How do you know?

3. What happened to the energy stored in the balls when you released them? How do you know?

4. Some materials can store energy as they change shape when striking a surface. Which material, rubber or clay, stores more energy this way? How do you know?

Steps 3 and 4

INVESTIGATE FURTHER!

EXPERIMENT

In this activity you discovered that a rubber ball bounces differently than does a clay ball. Now get together with your group members and design an experiment to find out how balls made of other materials respond to being dropped from different heights. You might also design an experiment to find out if the mass of a ball affects how high it will bounce. After you have designed your experiment and described it in writing, show it to your teacher. If your teacher approves, carry out your experiment and record your results.

Activity

Roller Coaster Energy

A roller coaster car has stored energy as it sits at the top of the first hill. How does the energy change as the car speeds down this hill and up the next?

MATERIALS

- aquarium tubing (about 3 m)
- BB or small marble
- masking tape
- *Science Notebook*

Procedure

1. Place a BB inside a piece of aquarium tubing and seal the ends of the tubing with tape.

2. Let the BB roll to one end of the tubing. Raise that end of the tubing and release the BB. **Observe** how its speed changes as it rolls down the tubing. **Record** your observations in your *Science Notebook*.

3. Arrange the tubing in a series of hills (at least two) to model the form of a roller coaster track. The beginning of your model should be the top of a hill. **Sketch your model** roller coaster in your *Science Notebook*.

4. Place the BB at the starting point of your model and release it. **Observe** and **record** how the speed of the BB changes as it moves through the tubing.

5. If the BB doesn't make it all the way to the end, reshape the tubing and try again.

Step 3

C16

Analyze and Conclude

1. Compare the potential energy of the BB with its energy of motion just after you released it.

2. At what point in its journey does the BB have the most energy of motion?

3. When does the BB speed up during its trip? When does it slow down?

4. When is the BB traveling the fastest in the tubing? When is it traveling the slowest?

5. The energy of the BB changes from stored energy to energy of motion as it travels through the tubing. Describe the BB's trip along your model roller coaster in terms of the energy changes that take place.

INVESTIGATE FURTHER!

EXPERIMENT

Shape the tubing so that it has a loop in it. First draw the shape of the track. Then experiment with the track until the BB can make it through the entire loop. What factor seems to determine whether the BB moves all the way through?

Energy Changes

▲ **All of these objects contain stored energy.**

Look at the pictures on this page. What do the sugar, the dynamite, and the skier at the top of a steep hill have in common? They all have energy stored in them.

Sugar is a source of quick energy that can help you do something like dash around a basketball court. Dynamite can blow rocks out of a mountainside. And when a skier moves onto the slope of a hill, he or she has enough energy to speed swiftly to the bottom of the hill.

So the sugar, the dynamite, and the poised skier contain enough energy to cause something to change position, or to move from one place to another. However, the energy in these things isn't being used. It's just sitting there, waiting for something to set it loose. This energy-in-waiting is called potential energy. **Potential energy** is stored energy.

Chemical Storehouses

Energy is stored in different ways. Consider a packet of sugar and a stick of dynamite. Although one of these materials is harmless and the other can be very destructive, both materials store energy in the same way.

The energy in sugar and dynamite is stored in the chemical bonds that link their atoms. A bond can be compared to the rope in a tug of war. The atoms are like people pulling on opposite ends of the rope. The energy the people exert is stored in the rope. The rope holds the people together. But if the rope breaks, the people go flying in opposite directions. When this happens, the energy that was stored in the rope is released.

When you eat sugar, the chemical bonds that

store energy in the sugar are broken down by chemicals in your body. This action releases energy for you to use. With dynamite, the bonds are broken down by a spark or a jolt of electricity. When these bonds break, a great deal of energy is released very quickly. Because the energy in sugar and dynamite is stored in chemical bonds, it is called chemical potential energy.

How Much Energy?

How much energy is stored in that packet of sugar you read about earlier? If you read the label on a packet, you'll find that the sugar contains 16 Calories. But what does that tell you about the amount of stored energy in the sugar?

A Calorie is a measure of energy. One Calorie is the amount of heat energy needed to raise the temperature of 1 kg of water 1°C. So if changed to heat energy, the stored energy in a packet of sugar could raise the temperature of 1 kg of water 16°C.

The Calorie is a useful unit for finding the stored energy in different foods. But scientists deal with many different forms of energy, and they need a unit of measure that can be applied to all of

▲ **Food is burned in a calorimeter (kal ə rim'ət ər) to find out how many Calories the food contains.**

them. The **joule** (jo͞ol) is the basic unit of energy used by scientists.

The joule is named after an English scientist who studied the relationship between heat and other forms of energy. One joule is the amount of energy that is needed to raise the temperature of 1 g of water 4.18°C.

Transfer of Energy

Look at the photograph on page C20. A couple of seconds before the picture was taken, the two acrobats on the end of the seesaw were standing up on the platform to their right. The acrobat flying through the air was standing on the other end of the seesaw.

Energy stored in the rope is released when the rope breaks. ▼

▲ Where did the flying acrobat's energy come from?

While standing on the platform, the two acrobats had potential energy because of their position above the ground. They had stored that energy as they climbed up to the platform. Energy stored in an object because of its position above the ground is called gravitational potential energy. Such an object can be set in motion by Earth's pull of gravity on the object.

As the two acrobats stepped off the platform, their potential energy was changed to kinetic (ki net'ik) energy. **Kinetic energy** is energy of motion. When the acrobats landed on the seesaw, their kinetic energy pushed one end of the seesaw down. The other end was pushed up, launching the third acrobat into the air. The kinetic energy of the two acrobats had been transferred through the seesaw to the third acrobat.

Energy on a Roller Coaster

The thrills of a roller coaster ride depend on repeated changes in energy—from potential to kinetic and back again. These changes are similar to the changes that the BB experienced as it moved through the plastic tubing in the activity on pages C16 and C17.

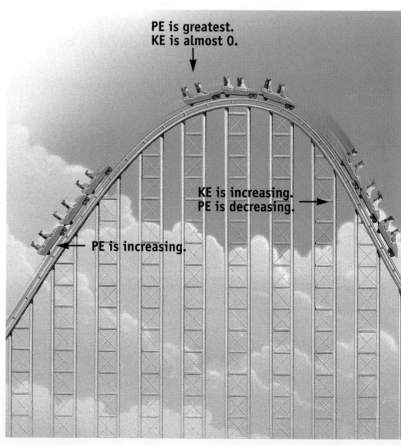

PE is greatest.
KE is almost 0.

KE is increasing.
PE is decreasing.

PE is increasing.

C20

As a roller coaster ride begins, energy supplied by a motor hauls the roller coaster car up a track. As the car goes up, it gains potential energy. At the top of the hill, when its potential energy is greatest, the car is set loose.

What happens now? The car begins to roll down the hill. It gains kinetic energy. The potential energy the car had due to its position at the top of the hill is changing to energy of motion.

As the seconds flash by, more and more potential energy is changed into kinetic energy. How do you know this is happening? The roller coaster moves faster and faster down the track.

When the car reaches the bottom of the hill, all the potential energy it had at the top of the hill has been changed to kinetic energy. At this point the car is moving so fast it has enough kinetic energy to carry it all the way up to the top of the next hill.

As the car climbs, it slows down. Kinetic energy is being changed back to potential energy. When the car reaches the top of the hill, it begins a new plunge. Once again, potential energy changes into kinetic energy. Engineers design roller coaster rides so that repeated changes from potential to kinetic energy and back to potential will keep the cars in motion for the entire trip. And the changes will keep you screaming all the way. ■

Energy changes in a roller coaster ride ▼

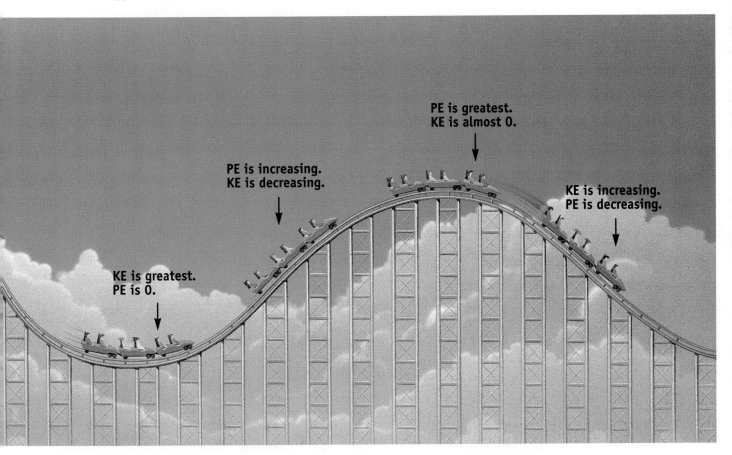

PE is greatest.
KE is almost 0.

PE is increasing.
KE is decreasing.

KE is increasing.
PE is decreasing.

KE is greatest.
PE is 0.

Green Plants: Energy Factories

Every country in the world is dotted with silent factories. In some places these factories cover the land as far as the eye can see. You may be thinking that these factories must be idle if they are silent, that no useful products are being made.

These factories, however, aren't idle—they make a product without which you and all the world's people could not live. That product is food. And the food contains the stored energy all living things need to carry out their life activities.

Unfortunately, in many countries of the world there aren't enough of these factories to keep all the people healthy or even alive. What's more, many scientists fear that the situation may get worse as the years pass. Later you'll find out why scientists think this is true. But first let's take a brief tour of one of these energy factories to find out what it is and how it works.

The factories are green plants. Green plants make their own food. That food is also used by all living things that eat green plants. The plants are not actually single factories. Rather, the plants contain millions of tiny factories called chloroplasts (klôr′ə plasts).

The chemical chlorophyll gives chloroplasts their green color. Inside a chloroplast, water from the soil and carbon dioxide from the air are combined

The product made in this factory is sugar. ▼

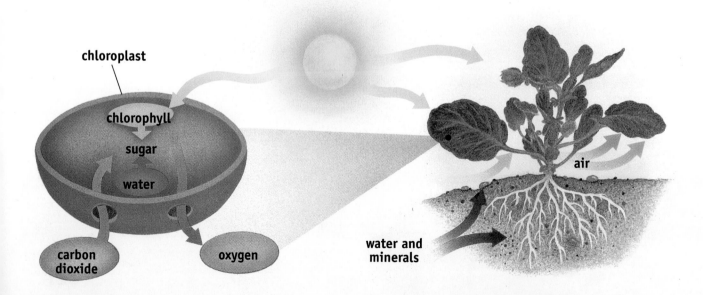

to make a sugar called glucose (glōō′kōs). In this process, called photosynthesis (fōt ō sin′thə sis), some of the sun's energy gets stored in the glucose.

When you eat a leaf of spinach, a slice of bread, or any other plant product, you're taking in energy stored in glucose. In your body, your cells are able to break down the glucose and release its stored energy. You're using some of that energy right now. You're using energy to move, to think, and to do all the other things that keep you alive.

This thought brings us back to the problem that faces many people—hunger! Of the almost 6 billion people in the world, more than half a billion don't get enough food. Many millions of people die every year from starvation.

In some places the human population is growing faster than farmers are able to grow the crops needed to feed the people. In a sense the energy factories aren't keeping up with the people factories. The reasons can be summed

▲ **Bad weather can lead to crop failures.**

up in a few words—bad weather, poor soil, and increasing populations.

Scientists and farmers all over the world are seeking solutions to the problem of hunger. New methods to increase crop production have been successful in some countries. But further efforts are needed to find ways to adequately feed all the people in the world. ■

INVESTIGATION 2

1. Trace the energy you get from eating an apple back to the Sun.

2. You give a friend on a playground swing one hard push. Describe the energy changes that the swing undergoes until it stops moving.

INVESTIGATION 3

WHAT ARE WORK AND FRICTION?

List all the work you've done since you got up today. A scientist's list might be quite different from yours. To a scientist, *work* has a special meaning. Check your list again after this investigation. Then you'll know how many of your activities involve "real" work and why work isn't easy.

Activity

A Lifting Experience

How much work do you do when you lift things? Take some measurements in this activity.

MATERIALS
- spring scale
- small cloth bag or plastic bag
- meterstick
- assorted objects to be weighed
- *Science Notebook*

Procedure

1. Make a chart in your *Science Notebook* like the one shown here.

Object	Force (Newtons)	Distance (Meters)	Work (Joules)

2. The force needed to lift an object is equal to the weight of the object. Weigh each object by placing it in a small bag and hanging the bag from a spring scale, as shown. Use the weight unit labeled *Newton* on the scale. Record the weights in your chart under the heading *Force*.

Step 2

3. Use a meterstick to **measure** the heights of two different tables in your classroom.

4. Place on the floor all of the objects you weighed. Lift half the objects onto the lower table. Then lift the rest of the objects onto the higher table. **Record** the height an object is lifted in the *Distance* column of your chart.

Step 4

5. Find the amount of work done on each object by multiplying the weight of an object by the distance you lifted it. **Record** the results in the *Work* column of your chart.

Analyze and Conclude

1. **Describe** the relationship between the weight of an object and the work you do to lift it.

2. **Describe** the relationship between the height that you lift an object and the work that you do to lift it.

3. Suppose you lift an object that weighs 3 newtons onto a shelf that is 2 m high. Then you lift an object weighing 6 newtons onto a bench that is 1 m high. How would the amount of work done on the first object compare with that done on the second object? How do you know?

Activity
Sliding Along

Sometimes when you have to move something that's too heavy or bulky to lift, you slide it along the floor. Then you notice that a force seems to push against you. Discover the nature of that force.

Procedure

1. Tack a piece of sandpaper to one half of the board, as shown.

2. Rub your finger across the smooth part of the board and then across the sandpaper. In your *Science Notebook*, **describe** the differences you feel.

3. Stick a tack in the top of one of the wooden blocks. Place the block on the board and loop the rubber band around the tack.

4. **Measure** and **record** the length of the unstretched rubber band. Then slowly pull on the rubber band until the block moves along the smooth part of the board at a steady speed. Have a group member **measure** and **record** how much the rubber band stretches as you pull the block.

Step 1

5. **Predict** how the sandpaper will affect how much the rubber band will stretch. Then pull the block across the sandpaper. **Measure** and **record** how much the rubber band stretches as the block is pulled.

6. Use string and thumbtacks to attach two wooden blocks, as shown. Use the rubber band to pull the blocks across a smooth surface—a desktop, for example. **Measure** and **record** how much the rubber band stretches as you pull the blocks.

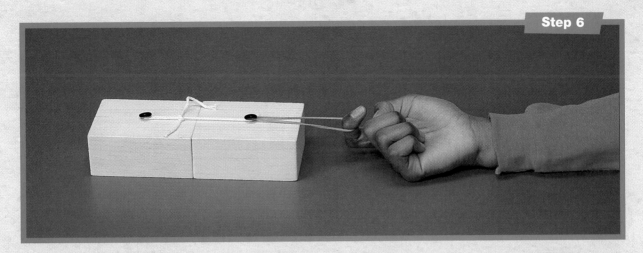

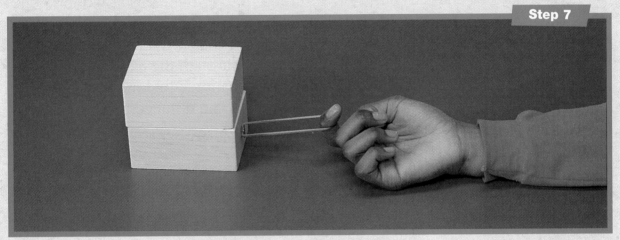

7. Now place one block on top of the other. Again, use the rubber band to pull the blocks along the smooth surface. **Measure** and **record** how much the rubber band stretches.

Analyze and Conclude

1. Does it take more force to move the block over the smooth surface or over the rough surface? **Tell what evidence** you used to draw your conclusion.

2. **Compare** the forces needed to move the blocks in steps 6 and 7. What is different about the two setups?

3. **Friction** is a force that opposes motion. What **inferences** can you make about friction, based on this activity?

UNIT PROJECT LINK

Each block used in the Great Pyramid of Giza was transported several kilometers over land and then moved up a sloping side of the pyramid. Design methods to decrease the effort needed to move each block by reducing friction between the block and the surface over which it moves.

When It's Work and
When It's Not

You might think that reading a difficult book is hard work. A scientist might say, "Well, it all depends." You might answer, "Depends on what?" "Depends on whether or not you turn the pages," the scientist would reply.

You see, the word *work* has a special meaning for scientists. Specifically, **work** is done if a force moves an object. If there's no movement, no work is done. So merely reading, no matter how difficult the subject matter, isn't work. On the other hand, turning the pages of a book *is* work.

When you turn a page, you apply a force to the page with your fingers. A **force** is a pull or push. That force moves the page a certain distance. The amount of work you do depends on the size of the force you exert on the page and the distance the page moves. This idea can be expressed by the statement: *Work equals force times distance.* Scientists use a shorthand formula to express the amount of work done. This formula is

$$W = F \times D$$

Energy and Work

Energy is needed to do work. For example, the energy released when dynamite explodes underground is transferred to the rocks as work is done on them by the force of the explosion. This force makes the rocks fly some distance through the air. So energy produces a force that moves an object through some distance. And that's doing work.

Getting Tired Without Doing Work

Imagine you and some friends are collecting large rocks to build a wall around a summer camp. You come upon a perfect rock in the middle of a narrow trail. You bend down and pull on the rock, but it doesn't move. You

No work is done. ▼

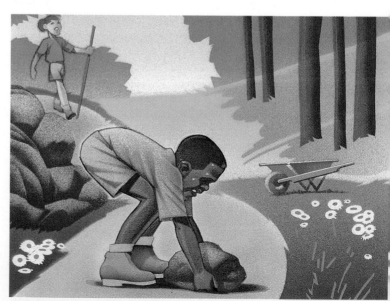

get a better grip and pull even harder, but still no luck.

You don't give up. You keep pulling, your muscles begin to ache, and sweat begins to roll down your head and into your eyes. Finally, you can't pull anymore. You've used up a lot of energy, and you're very tired. But you still haven't done any work on the rock. The force you exerted on the rock didn't move it any distance.

While you're catching your breath from your exertion, a friend comes along and offers to help you move the rock. Acting together, the two of you are able to exert enough force to lift the rock. Once the rock has been lifted, your friend tells you to hold it while she goes for the wheelbarrow you left at the side of the trail.

You get a good grip on the rock and your friend lets go. And you hang on for dear life! Although it only takes your friend a few seconds to get the wheelbarrow and bring it back, it seems like forever. By the time you lower the rock into the wheelbarrow, your muscles are shaking and your knees are weak.

Surely you did some work on the rock while you were holding it. Wrong again! Even though you exerted a lot of force to keep the rock from falling, you didn't move the rock. Once again, you're tired and sore, but you didn't do any work on the rock.

How Work Is Measured

As you discovered earlier, work can be calculated by multiplying the force exerted on an object by the distance the object moves, or $W = F \times D$.

You know how distance is measured. You measure distance in a familiar unit called the meter (m). But you may not be familiar with the unit used to measure force. This unit is called a **newton** (N). Scientists named this unit in honor of Sir Isaac Newton, a famous British scientist who studied force and motion about 300 years ago.

Since force and distance units are multiplied to get work, the unit for work turns out to be the newton-meter (N-m). You might think this is a clumsy unit.

Work is done. ▼

No work is done. ▼

And scientists have agreed with you. They simplified the unit by calling it a joule (J). Recall that a joule is a unit for measuring energy. Since doing work on an object transfers energy to the object, it makes sense to measure both work and energy in the same unit.

Now you can figure out how much work you and your friend did in lifting the rock 1 m. Let's say that the rock weighed 200 newtons.

Use the formula:

$$W = F \times D$$
$$= 200\ N \times 1\ m$$
$$= 200\ N\text{-}m,\ or\ 200\ J$$

How much work would you and your friend have done if the rock had weighed 250 N and was lifted 0.5 m above the ground? Figure it out.

Why Doing Work Isn't Easy

To get any work done, you always have to overcome some force. For example, gravity is a force you have to overcome to lift something. Friction is another force you have to overcome to do work, especially when you're trying to move an object along the ground. You learned about friction in the activity on pages C26 and C27.

Friction and gravity are forces that resist, or oppose, certain motions. Forces that resist motion are called **resistance forces**. The force you have to exert on an object to get it to move is called the **effort force**. In order for work to be done on an object, the effort force must always be greater than the resistance force. ■

SCIENCE IN LITERATURE

RACING THE IDITAROD TRAIL
by Ruth Crisman
Dillon Press, 1993

Sled dog racing is a popular sport in the state of Alaska. Most people would probably consider sled dog racing to be more work than sport. To find out why, read pages 27-29 of *Racing the Iditarod Trail* by Ruth Crisman. You'll learn about the rigorous training schedule followed by both dogs and "mushers," as sled dog drivers are called.

Then read about an actual race. Imagine the stored energy in the muscles of the dogs changing to mechanical energy of the moving sleds. Think about the amount of work they accomplish in pulling a loaded sled over the 1,600-km course. Is there any doubt that sled dogs are among the best-conditioned athletes in the world?

Friction and Work

You're speeding down a snow-covered hill on a toboggan. As you near the bottom of the hill, you expect to slow down and come to a stop. But to your surprise and amazement, your toboggan doesn't slow down. It keeps on moving at a constant speed over long stretches of flat ground.

Towns and cities flash by. You cross one state border after another. The snow is gone, but your toboggan keeps gliding over grass, sand, concrete, and gravel. You wonder if you will ever stop moving. And you won't—the force of friction has been suspended!

Suddenly, the sound of your alarm clock intrudes into your fantasy. Your dream is over, and friction is back.

▲ . . . sometimes it's not!

Friction: The Antimotion Force

A world without friction is only possible in a dream or a science fiction story. Any time that matter rubs against other matter, there is friction.

The matter could be any of these things: the runners of a sled and the snow under them, the soles of your shoes and a sidewalk, the tires of a car and the concrete of a road.

Friction is a force that acts against other forces, like pushes and pulls. Since pushes and pulls tend to produce motion, you might think of friction as being an antimotion force. *Anti-* means "against" or "opposed to."

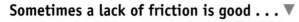
Sometimes a lack of friction is good . . . ▼

C31

If there were no friction, walking would be impossible. And if, somehow, you did manage to get yourself moving, how would you stop? You couldn't grab onto anything, because grabbing requires friction. You'd have to crash into something, like a fence or a tree.

As you can see, there are times when friction is useful. There are also times when it is not. It's not useful if you want to glide a long way on a sled. It's very useful, however, if you want to play basketball without falling down every time you cut toward the basket. And, of course, it's extremely useful if you want to stop a moving car.

The Friction Story Heats Up

Friction slows a moving object by changing some of its kinetic energy to heat energy. That is, the energy of motion is changed to heat energy. This heat is wasted energy. As more of a moving object's kinetic energy is turned to heat, the slower the object moves.

How do you know that friction produces heat? If you've ever seen a speeding car screech to a stop, you may have seen a puff of smoke and smelled something unpleasant. The smoke came from the car's tires rubbing against the road. And burning rubber has an unpleasant smell.

But you don't have to recall a near accident to experience the heat produced by friction. Just rub your hands together. What do you feel?

Friction: More or Less

It's a cold winter day and your front walk is a sheet of ice. You have friends coming over, and you're afraid that someone might slip on the ice and get hurt. So you go out and spread some sand over the ice.

Recall how the sandpaper in the activity on pages C26 and C27 increased the friction between the blocks and the board. Spreading sand over the walk will make the surface of

Friction at work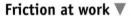

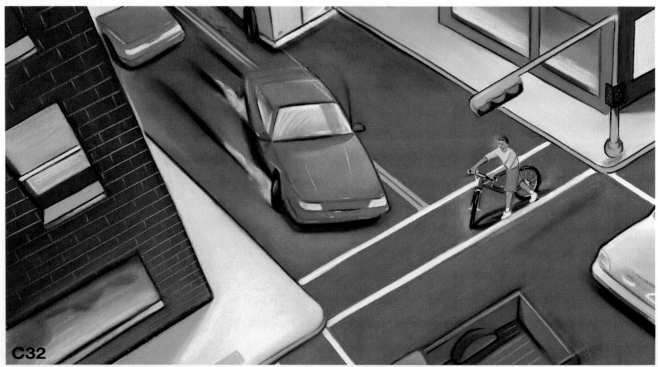

▲ **Sliding friction can be difficult to overcome.**

the ice rougher. This will increase the friction between your friends' feet and the ice, thereby making the ice less slippery.

Now let's change seasons. It's spring and you've been asked by your parents to haul a carton of trash to the curb. The carton is too bulky to carry, so you try pushing and pulling it across the ground. The carton barely budges.

After a few minutes of shoving and hauling, you decide that there's too much friction between the carton and the ground. You're up against something called sliding friction. How can you reduce this friction?

You think for awhile and come up with an idea. You put the carton on a skateboard and push. The carton moves easily. How come? You substituted rolling friction for sliding friction. And rolling friction produces less resistance to motion because the surface areas that rub together are much smaller.

Wheels, rollers, and ball bearings are all used to reduce sliding friction. Imagine trying to move a freight train without wheels, and you'll get a clear idea of the advantages of rolling friction over sliding friction.

Skating on Water

Another way to reduce sliding friction is to place some fluid between the surfaces that rub against each other. *Lubricants* (lōō′bri-kəntz), such as oil, grease, and wax are probably the most familiar fluids used to reduce friction. For example, you can apply wax to the runners of a sticky drawer, or oil to a squeaky hinge. In addition to making work easier, lubricants extend the life of moving parts of machines that rub against other parts.

You can roll along with rolling friction. ▼

▲ **This girl is skating on "thin water."**

You probably think that ice is slippery enough, right? Well, if you've ever been ice skating, your skate blades have actually made the ice even more slippery. As the blades of your skates slide across the ice, heat is produced. This heat melts the ice beneath your skate blades. So the blades glide over a thin film of water. This fluid lubrication reduces the friction between the blades of your skates and the ice.

Friction and Work

You know from experience that it takes more force to slide an object over a rough surface than over a smooth one. You also know that rough surfaces produce more friction than smooth surfaces. So you can infer that it takes extra force to overcome friction. How does this need for extra force affect the amount of work you do?

For a clue to the answer to this question, take another look at the formula for work—$W = F \times D$. This formula tells you that the work done in moving an object is equal to the force used times the distance the object is moved. What happens if friction makes you exert extra force to move the object? You have to do more work to move the object the same distance.

Friction, then, is sort of a mixed bag. Friction can make work harder, and it can wear out your shoes. But friction also makes moving about possible. And without it, you couldn't lick an ice-cream cone. ■

INVESTIGATION 3

1. Explain why you wouldn't wear basketball shoes to go bowling.

2. Imagine that you pick up a book from the floor and place it on a shelf 1.5 m high. If the book has a weight of 10 N, how much work do you do?

REFLECT & EVALUATE

WORD POWER

conduction   convection
effort forces   energy
force   joule
work   newton
radiation
potential energy
resistance forces
kinetic energy

 On Your Own
Write a definition for each term in the list.

 With a Partner
Make up a quiz, using all the terms in the list. Challenge your partner to complete the quiz.

Cut out a picture of a roller coaster from a magazine, or draw your own roller coaster. Glue your picture to a sheet of posterboard. Add labels to your poster to show how a roller coaster makes use of potential energy and kinetic energy.

Analyze Information

Study the drawings. Then use the drawings to explain how much work each person will do in moving their rock the distance shown.

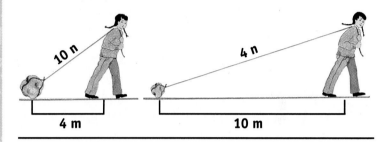

Assess Performance

Design an experiment to determine the effect of oil on friction. Work with the materials you used in the "Sliding Along" activity and salad oil. Predict how the oil will affect friction. Then conduct your experiment and check your prediction.

Problem Solving

1. Samantha used a match to light the candles on her brother's birthday cake. Describe all the energy changes that were involved. What role did potential energy play in the lighting of the candles?

2. Suppose you put a pot of water on the stove to boil. Describe how heat is transferred from the stove burner to the water.

3. Imagine that you pick up a carton of books that weighs 20 N and lift it to a height of 1 m. You carry it 12 m across the room and place it on a shelf 2 m high. How much work do you do on the carton of books?

CHAPTER 2

WORK AND MACHINES

Some words just go together: *salt* and *pepper, day* and *night, hot* and *cold, on* and *off*. What words seem to go with *knife, hammer*, and *tennis racket*? You might answer *fork, nails*, and *tennis ball*. However, in this chapter you'll find *one* word that goes with *knife, hammer*, and *tennis racket*. That word is *machine*.

What a Racket

During a two-week period that begins in late August, the U.S. Open Tennis Championships are held at the National Tennis Center in New York City. This tournament features the top tennis players in the world. Among them is Zina Garrison Jackson, a professional American tennis player who is among the very best. To play tennis at Zina's level, an athlete must have stamina, quickness, and the ability to hit a tennis ball with great accuracy. Of course, one other item is essential: A TENNIS RACKET!

Through countless hours of practice, Zina Garrison Jackson has developed techniques for hitting winning shots with power and precision. She has mastered the machine of tennis. That's right—a tennis racket is a type of simple machine known as a lever. In this chapter, you'll learn how levers and other machines help you do work.

Coming Up

◄ Zina Garrison Jackson,
tennis professional

HOW DO RAMPS HELP US DO WORK?

Imagine that you are planning to hike to the top of a mountain, and you have the choice of two trails. One trail winds around the mountain at a gentle slope to the top; the other follows a straight path up the side of the mountain. Both trails start at the same point and end at the same place. Yet one trail is much easier to climb. Why? Which trail would you take?

Activity

Ramps and Rocks

The mountain trails are types of ramps. Suppose that, after returning from your hike, you had to move a heavy rock from the ground onto the back of a truck. Would it be easier to lift the rock straight up or slide it up a ramp?

MATERIALS

- string
- small rock
- paper clip
- thin rubber band
- metric ruler
- smooth board
- 3 books
- *Science Notebook*

Procedure

1. Tie a piece of string around a small rock. Bend a paper clip into a double hook. Connect it to the rock, as shown.

2. Measure the length of an un-stretched rubber band and **record** the length in your *Science Notebook*. Hook the rubber band to the paper clip and rock. Use the rubber band to lift the rock. Have a group member measure and record the length of the stretched rubber band.

Step 1

3. Make a ramp by placing one end of a smooth board on a pile of books. Place the rock at the bottom of the ramp.

4. Predict how much the rubber band will stretch when you pull the rock up the ramp. Slowly pull on the rubber band until the rock starts to move up the ramp. Continue to pull at a slow, steady rate so that the rubber band remains stretched at a constant length. Have a group member **measure** and **record** how far the rubber band stretches as you pull on it.

Analyze and Conclude

1. What force does the stretching of the rubber band measure?

2. How do you know that you are doing work in step 1 and in step 4?

3. Did you have to exert more force to lift the rock or to pull it up the ramp? Explain your answer.

4. How does using a ramp make the job of raising a heavy object easier?

INVESTIGATE FURTHER!

....

RESEARCH

Look for a construction project underway around your school or neighborhood. See if a ramp is in use there. Prepare a report explaining how the ramp is being used.

Step 4

Activity

Different Slants on Doing Work

Some ramps are steeper than others. How does a ramp's steepness affect the force needed to move things along it?

MATERIALS

- metric ruler
- 3 books
- 3 boards of different lengths
- small heavy object
- small cart with wheels
- spring scale
- *Science Notebook*

Procedure

1. In your *Science Notebook*, make a chart like the one shown here.

Length of Ramp	Height of Books	Force

2. Measure the lengths of the three boards. Record these lengths in the first column of your chart. Stack three books. Measure and record the height of the stack.

3. Use the longest board to make a ramp up to the top of the stack of books.

4. Place the object to be moved in a cart, and use a spring scale to pull the cart up the ramp at a steady speed, as shown. Have a group member observe the reading on the spring scale and record it in the *Force* column of your chart.

5. Predict what effect the use of shorter boards would have on the force needed to pull the cart up the ramps. To check your prediction, repeat step 4, using the other boards as ramps.

Analyze and Conclude

1. Make a bar graph of your data. Plot ramp lengths on the *x*-axis and plot force along the *y*-axis.

2. Describe the relationship between the length of a ramp and the force needed to move a load up the ramp.

3. What is the advantage of using a ramp with a gentle slope? a steeper slope?

Step 4

Activity

Ramp with a Twist

Long ramps take up a lot of room. But can a long ramp be redesigned so that it takes up less space?

MATERIALS

- metric ruler
- crayon or colored pencil
- sheet of unlined paper
- scissors
- tape
- unsharpened pencil
- screw
- *Science Notebook*

Procedure

1. With a ruler and a crayon, draw a diagonal line across a sheet of paper from corner to corner. Cut the paper along this diagonal and keep one triangle.

2. Notice that the colored line is like a ramp. Measure the length of this line and record the length of the line in your *Science Notebook*.

3. Brainstorm with members of your group to come up with a way to make the line on the paper produce a "ramp" that winds around a pencil. Then carry out your plan. In your notebook, draw a sketch of your model ramp.

Step 3

4. Measure and record the length of the pencil.

5. Compare the ramp on the pencil with the threads on a screw.

Analyze and Conclude

1. How does the length of the diagonal line compare with the length of the pencil? How did you make the "ramp" take up less space?

2. Which part of the screw is similar to the ramp that winds around the pencil?

3. When a screw is twisted down into a board, what "travels" along the ramp part of the screw?

A Barrier-Free
Environment

The next time you're out walking around your community, notice where there are ramps. In many cities and towns, the curbs at street corners are gentle ramps rather than steps. And gently sloping ramps lead from streets to the entrances of theaters, schools, office buildings, and other public places.

In such cases, steps have been replaced by ramps to make it easier for people in wheelchairs to get around. The ramps have also proved to be a great help for people pushing wheeled vehicles such as shopping carts and strollers.

Some buildings have ramps inside, as well as stairs. An example of a building famous for its ramps is the Solomon R. Guggenheim Museum in New York City. A great spiral ramp encircles the inside of this unusual building, which is home to the works of many of the world's great modern artists.

▲ **Inside the Guggenheim Museum**

As you might guess, engineers who design ramps for people in wheelchairs must make sure that the slopes of such ramps are gradual enough to allow wheelchair users to comfortably climb the ramp. To accomplish this, engineers have found that a ramp must be ten times as long as the height to which it climbs. You could also say that for every meter a ramp rises, it must be 10 meters long. ■

INVESTIGATE FURTHER!

TAKE ACTION

Let's say you're an engineer. You're asked to design a ramp to be installed beside a staircase. The staircase rises 3 m from one floor to the next. How long must you make the ramp? What if the foot of the staircase is too close to a wall for you to make a ramp as long as you need it to be? How might you redesign the ramp? Hint: Think Guggenheim.

Simple Machines

The place is Africa. The time is 2 million years ago. A hunter crouches over an antelope he has just killed. The hunter begins to skin the animal with a sharpened rock. A short distance away, a second hunter uses a stone ax to chop a slender branch from a tree. He will make a spear from the branch.

The First Machines

The sharpened rocks used by these early hunters are tools. They are the first machines invented by humans. A **machine** is a device that makes work easier. One way that some machines make work easier is by reducing the amount of force needed to do a job. In effect, such machines multiply the force you apply to them.

Inclined Planes

The sharpened edge of each stone tool is a type of inclined plane. An

▲ Ancient stone tools were the earliest machines

inclined plane is a simple machine with a sloping surface. A ramp is a familiar example of an inclined plane. As you learned in the activity on pages C38 and C39, it is easier to raise objects from one level to another using a ramp than it is to simply lift the objects directly.

Look at the drawings below. Use the drawings and your observations from the activity, "Different Slants on Doing Work," to infer the answer to the caption question.

A.

B.

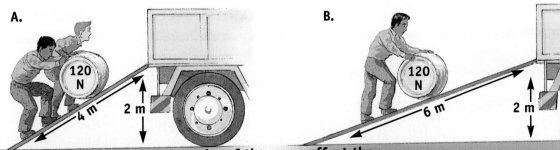

120 N
4 m
2 m

120 N
6 m
2 m

▲ How does the slope, or angle, of the ramp affect the force needed to move the barrel up to the platform?

Sometimes it isn't practical to use a straight inclined plane to do a job. For example, suppose you wanted to ride your trail bike to a campsite at the top of the mountain shown in the picture. Both trails are ramps. Which trail would make the job of pedaling up to the campsite easier?

Inclined Planes That Move

A wedge is a special type of inclined plane that moves. Wedges are used to push objects or materials apart. Recall the stone tools used by the hunters on page C43. The edges of such tools are examples of wedges.

A screw is another example of an inclined plane that moves. When a screw is driven into a board, the wood actually travels along the threads of the screw. A screw can also be used to raise or lower something, like the seat of a piano stool.

One Advantage of Using a Machine

A machine helps to make work easier. A machine does not, however, reduce the *amount* of work that is done. Look again at the drawings on page C43. The work being accomplished is moving the barrel from the ground onto the truck.

▲ A wedge is two inclined planes placed back-to-back. What part of a screw is like an inclined plane?

Using the formula $W = F \times D$, the amount of work required to lift the barrel straight up can be calculated as

120 N × 2 m = 240 N × m, or 240 joules

The amount of force needed to move the barrel up either of the ramps is less than 120 N. However, the force is exerted through a greater distance. Because of friction, you will do more work when you use a machine than when you don't use one! The actual work done when you move the barrel up either ramp is greater than 240 joules!

A machine doesn't reduce the amount of work done, but it does help make work easier. An inclined plane is one type of machine that makes it possible to reduce the force a person needs to exert in doing work.

The number of times that a machine multiplies the effort force is called the **mechanical advantage** (MA) of the machine. To find the mechanical advantage of an inclined plane (while ignoring friction), divide the length of its sloping surface by its height.

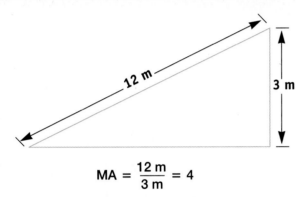

$$MA = \frac{12 \text{ m}}{3 \text{ m}} = 4$$

In drawing *A* on page C43, the length of the inclined plane is 4 m and its height is 2 m. So the mechanical advantage of this inclined plane is

$$MA = \frac{4 \text{ m}}{2 \text{ m}} = 2$$

◀ **Can you think of any *disadvantage* in using the winding trail?**

This inclined plane multiplies the effort force two times. So by using it, the workers exert about one-half as much force to move the barrel up onto the platform as they would have used to lift the barrel straight up. Keep in mind that the mechanical advantage is really a bit less than 2—friction makes it impossible to have a maximum mechanical advantage.

Now find the mechanical advantage of the inclined plane in drawing *B* on page C43. Would you have to exert more force to move the barrel using this ramp or the other ramp?

The advantage of using a ramp to raise an object is that you can use less force. Is there any disadvantage? Like the winding mountain trail, the disadvantage is you have to travel a greater distance. The gentler the slope of a ramp, the longer the ramp must be.

The next time you use an inclined plane, keep in mind that you're making your work easier. You may end up doing a little more work, but you won't need to use as much force to do it. ■

━━━━━━━ **INVESTIGATION 1** ━━━━━━━

1. How much work must you do to move a box of books weighing 2 N from the floor onto a shelf 0.8 m above the floor?

2. You use a ramp 4 m long to move the box of books onto the shelf. How does the ramp help you? How does it affect the actual amount of work you do? Explain.

WHAT ARE LEVERS AND PULLEYS?

Imagine that you are rowing across a lake. You pull on the oars in one direction, and the rowboat moves in the opposite direction. An oar is a type of simple machine called a lever. You might be surprised at the number of levers you use every day.

Activity

The Ups and Downs of a Seesaw

A seesaw is a type of lever. To make your end of the seesaw go up, you need someone to push down on the other end. How much force does that person have to use? Where should he or she sit? Let's find the answers to these questions.

Procedure

1. Tape three pencils together to make a triangle, as shown. Tape a paper cup to each end of a metric ruler.

2. Place the ruler on the pencils so that the middle of the ruler (the 15-cm mark) rests on the top of the triangle. You have made a lever. The point where the ruler touches the pencils is called the **fulcrum**.

3. Place a piece of clay the size of a large marble in the cup attached to the zero end of the ruler.

4. Add paper clips, one at a time, to the cup at the other end until the zero end of the ruler is lifted.

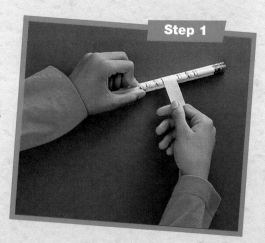

Step 1

5. In your *Science Notebook*, **make a chart** with two columns. In the first column, **record** the distance between the cup of paper clips and the fulcrum; in the second column, **record** the number of paper clips needed to lift the clay.

6. Take the paper clips out of the cup. Move the ruler so that the fulcrum is at the 10-cm mark of the ruler. Repeat step 4 and **record** the data.

7. Take the paper clips out of the cup and move the fulcrum to the 5-cm mark. **Predict** how many paper clips it will take to lift the cup containing the clay. **Record** your prediction; then repeat step 4 and **record** the data.

Analyze and Conclude

1. Describe the relationship between the distance of the clay from the fulcrum and the number of paper clips needed to lift the clay.

2. Talk with members of your group and **predict** how many paper clips you would need if the fulcrum were at the 8-cm mark. Then check your prediction.

3. Predict how many paper clips you would need if the fulcrum were at the 20-cm mark. Try the experiment and check your prediction.

4. What can you **infer** about how a lever makes the job of lifting the clay ball easier?

INVESTIGATE FURTHER!

EXPERIMENT

Suppose you and a friend are going to ride on a seesaw. Predict how you would adjust your position on the seesaw if you were using it with a friend who weighs less than you do. How about if your friend weighs more than you do? The next time you're on the playground, check your predictions.

Step 3

C47

Activity

The Pulley—A Special Kind of Lever

Have you ever raised a flag to the top of a flagpole? How did you get the flag up there? How did you get it down?

MATERIALS

- several books
- wooden ruler
- single pulley
- heavy string or twine
- small heavy object
- spring scale
- *Science Notebook*

Procedure

1. **Study** the pulley setup shown and **discuss** it with the members of your group.

2. Use the materials listed above to **set up** a similar pulley. A pulley arranged this way is known as a single fixed pulley. **Sketch** this arrangement in your *Science Notebook*.

3. Use a spring scale to **measure** the weight of a small heavy object. **Record** the weight.

4. Tie one end of a piece of heavy string to the heavy object. Place the object on the floor below the pulley. Thread the other end of the string through the pulley and tie it to the spring scale, as shown below.

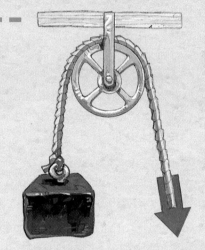

Step 4

5. **Predict** what will happen to the object if you pull down on the spring scale. Gently pull down on the spring scale and use the pulley to lift the object at a steady speed. **Record** the reading that is on the scale.

6. Remove the pulley from the ruler. Rearrange the pulley, string, and object as shown in the pictures. This arrangement is known as a single movable pulley.

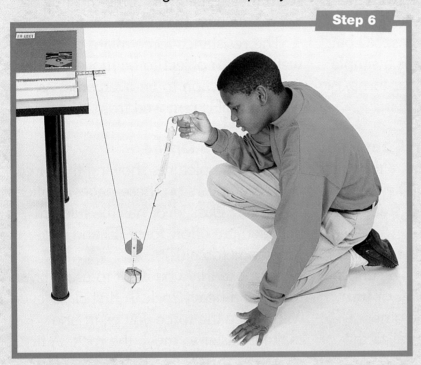

Step 6

7. Gently lift up on the spring scale, again using the pulley to lift the object. **Record** the reading on the scale.

Analyze and Conclude

1. When you used a fixed pulley, in what direction did you pull on the string? In what direction did the object move?

2. **Compare** the weight of the object with the force you used to lift the object with a fixed pulley.

3. **Compare** the weight of the object with the force you used to lift it with a movable pulley.

4. How did each pulley arrangement help you do work on the object?

INVESTIGATE FURTHER!

RESEARCH

Look around your school for pulleys. Investigate flagpoles and blinds in particular. Write a description of the pulleys you find. Include sketches to show how the pulleys operate.

Levers

If you've ever pried a rock from the ground with a crowbar, moved dirt with a wheelbarrow, or swung a baseball bat, you've used a lever. A **lever** is a simple machine made up of a bar that turns, or pivots, around a fixed point.

What All Levers Have in Common

Basically all levers are bars, although they don't all look like bars. The fixed point around which the bar is free to move is called the **fulcrum**.

You apply a force called the effort force on one part of a lever. The effort force causes the lever to pivot, or turn, around the fulcrum. At some other point on the lever is a force called the

resistance force. This force must be overcome if work is to be done.

The resistance force might be the weight of an object to be moved, or it might be friction to be overcome, as when a nail is removed from a board.

How Levers Differ

Study the pictures showing the three classes of levers on these pages. Notice that a first-class lever has the fulcrum between the effort force (E) and the resistance force (R).

Suppose that you want to use a lever to move a heavy rock. A first-class lever will reduce the force you exert and make it easier to move the rock. A first-

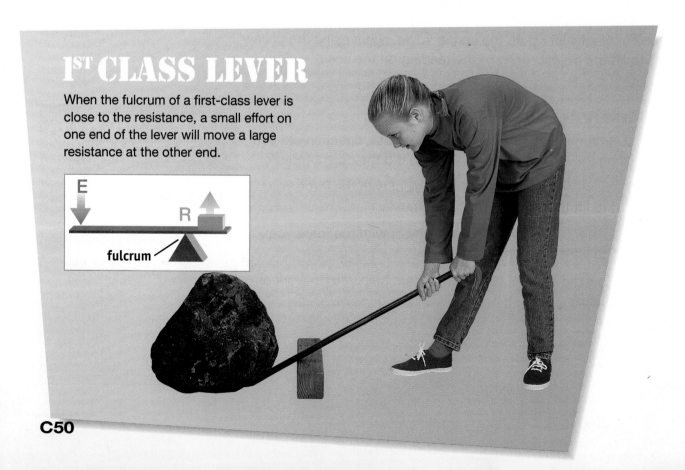

1ST CLASS LEVER

When the fulcrum of a first-class lever is close to the resistance, a small effort on one end of the lever will move a large resistance at the other end.

E
R
fulcrum

class lever also changes the direction of the force. However, the effort force must be exerted through a large distance to move the resistance a small distance.

In a second-class lever, the resistance force is between the fulcrum and the effort force. A second-class lever can reduce the force you have to exert, but it can't change the direction of that force. Notice that the nail shown will move in the same direction as the effort force.

In a third-class lever, the effort is exerted between the resistance and the fulcrum. A third-class lever does not reduce the force you exert or change its direction.

2ND CLASS LEVER

A hammer that is used to pull a nail from a board is an example of a second-class lever. As shown in the picture, the effort force is exerted at the end of the handle. The fulcrum is located where the hammerhead turns against the board. The resistance is offered by the nail. What causes this resistance force?

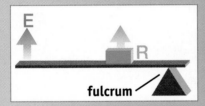

3RD CLASS LEVER

When the player pushes the hockey stick, she exerts the effort through a short distance. The curved end of the stick moves a greater distance. This means that the resistance force moves farther and faster than the effort force. This advantage can be used to make an object, such as a field hockey ball, move away from the stick at great speed.

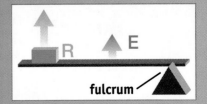

▲ **Bottle opener**

▲ **Wheelbarrow**

▲ **Oars**

Look at the picture of the field hockey player on page C51. When the player pushes on the stick, she exerts a strong effort force that doesn't move very far. The curved end of the stick exerts a force on the ball. This resistance force is not as strong as the effort force, but it moves much farther and faster than the effort force moves.

You use different kinds of levers every day, often without thinking about it. The pictures above show a variety of ways that people use levers to make their work easier to do. Study the pictures and identify the class of lever shown in each. ■

SCIENCE IN LITERATURE

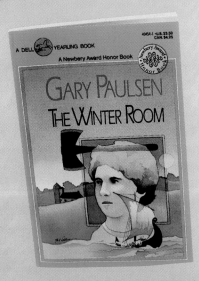

THE WINTER ROOM
by Gary Paulsen
A Yearling Book, Dell Publishing, 1991

In spring his brother uses a chisel and hammer to carve his name in a tree trunk. In summer his father takes the plow to be sharpened. In fall they use a pulley and rope to pull a slaughtered steer up to the ceiling. In winter his Uncle David told amazing stories. One was about a woodcutter. "It was said that no man could use an ax like him. The wood of the handle seemed to grow out of his hands, and there was nothing he could not do."

The winter room is where the farm families of long ago spent their waking time on long dark evenings. Through the eyes of a Minnesota farm boy, observe the change of seasons and their relationships to simple machines when you enjoy *The Winter Room* by Gary Paulsen.

How can you move a bag of cement from the ground to a roof 10 m above your head without moving your feet? Sounds impossible, doesn't it? But there is a simple machine that can make what seems like an impossible task possible. The simple machine is a pulley.

A **pulley** is a wheel around which a rope or chain is passed. If you attach an object to one end of the rope or chain and pull down on the other end, you can lift the object. And you can do this without moving your feet.

A Single Fixed Pulley

The drawing below shows a single fixed pulley similar to the one you set up in the activity on pages C48 and C49. The word *fixed* means that the pulley can't change position. It is attached to one place. In the drawing, the bag of cement is the resistance. A person is supplying the effort by pulling down on the rope.

A single fixed pulley is similar to a first-class lever with its fulcrum halfway between the effort and the resistance. In a pulley, the wheel is the fulcrum, and the rope supports the resistance that is to be moved.

A single fixed pulley doesn't change the effort force. It changes the direction of the force. When you pull down on the rope, the bag of cement goes up. This is certainly easier than carrying the bag of cement up a staircase.

A Single Movable Pulley

Do you recall the other single pulley you set up in the activity on pages C48 and 49? As shown in the drawing below, the arrangement of this pulley is different from that of the single fixed pulley just discussed. The pulley below is free to move. It is a single movable pulley. One end of the rope is fixed, and the other end is loose. If a person pulls on the loose end of the rope, the

A single fixed pulley ▼

A single movable pulley ▼

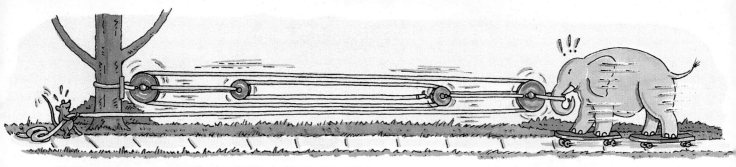

▲ **You'd be surprised how much work can be done with the right pulley combination.**

pulley and the bag of cement will move in the same direction as the effort force. In this case, the person pulls up, and the pulley and the cement both rise toward the roof.

What advantage is there to using such a pulley? It cuts the effort force exerted in half. This force is halved because the cement is supported by two lengths of rope instead of one.

What price do you pay for cutting the effort force in half? You have to exert that force through twice the distance that the resistance moves. In this case, for every meter that you raise the cement, you have to pull 2 m of rope through the pulley.

Pulley Combinations

The drawings at the bottom of the page show pulley systems that reduce effort three times, four times, and seven times. You can tell how much a pulley system will reduce effort by counting the lengths of rope that support the resistance. However, you don't always count the "effort" rope—the length of rope you're pulling on.

You only count the effort rope when the effort is exerted in the same direction that the resistance is moved. So if you pull down on a length of rope to lift a resistance, you don't count that length of rope.

Look at the pulley system below that reduces the effort three times. This system has two fixed pulleys and one movable pulley. The resistance moves in the opposite direction to the effort force. So you count the three ropes supporting the resistance, but not the effort rope.

To reduce the effort force by four, you would need a system that has four lengths of rope supporting the resistance.

Pulley combinations ▼

MA = 3

MA = 4

MA = 7

The pulley system shown in the middle is such a system.

Distance Makes the Difference

As the picture at the right shows, machines make it possible to do certain tasks that would be very difficult to accomplish otherwise. Because machines make work easier, it often seems as if they reduce the amount of work that is done.

If you ever find yourself thinking that a machine reduces work, recall this formula: $W = F \times D$. If you discount friction, W doesn't change when using a machine. For example, the work done in raising the piano from the ground to the window is always the same, no matter how you get it up there.

Most machines reduce the amount of force you have to exert to do work. To get this reduction, you sacrifice distance. So, if the F in the formula gets smaller, the D gets bigger, and W stays the same. For every meter that the workers raise the piano, they have to pull 4 m of rope through the pulley system.

Sometimes it takes longer to get work done using a machine. But distance and time are small prices to pay to get a job done. After all, how else are

▲ **Lifting a heavy object is no problem with a combination of pulleys.**

you going to get that big, heavy piano from the sidewalk up to the second floor of that apartment building? ■

INVESTIGATION 2

1. How is a single fixed pulley like a first-class lever? How are the two machines different?

2. You use a wheelbarrow to remove a pile of rocks from a vacant lot. What class of lever is the wheelbarrow? How do you know?

INVESTIGATION 3

WHAT IS A WHEEL AND AXLE?

Suppose someone removed the handlebars from your bicycle. Could you turn the front wheel by gripping the small shaft your handlebars were attached to? How do the handlebars help you do work on the front wheel?

Activity

Wheel and Axle

In this activity you'll find out how a wheel and axle work together to make a machine.

Procedure

1. Draw a circle with a diameter of 6 cm on a piece of posterboard. Cut it out and use the scissors to make a small hole in the center of the circle.

2. Insert a pencil through the hole in the center of the circle. The pencil is now the axle of your wheel and axle. Mark one point on the edge of the wheel.

Step 2

MATERIALS

- goggles
- drawing compass
- ruler
- posterboard
- scissors
- round pencil
- screwdriver
- screw in a board
- *Science Notebook*

SAFETY

Wear goggles. Use caution when working with scissors, screwdriver, and compass.

C56

3. Roll the wheel along the table top. Notice that the pencil turns once when the wheel turns once.

4. In your *Science Notebook*, **measure** and **record** the distance that the wheel travels in making one complete turn along the table top.

5. Remove the pencil from the wheel and roll the pencil on the table. **Measure** and **record** how far it travels in one complete turn.

6. Now grip a screwdriver by its metal shaft. Try to remove a screw from a board while gripping the screwdriver in this way.

Step 6

Step 7

7. Repeat step 6 while gripping the screwdriver by its handle, as shown.

Analyze and Conclude

1. How does the circumference of the posterboard wheel **compare** with that of the pencil "axle"? [Hint: You determined the circumference of each in steps 4 and 5.]

2. Suppose you were to grip the pencil axle and use it to turn the posterboard wheel. Through what distance would the axle have to turn to make a half-turn of the wheel? How does this type of machine help do work?

3. **Compare** the diameter of the screwdriver handle with the diameter of the shaft. Which is the wheel and which is the axle? Was it easier to turn the screw when you gripped the screwdriver by its shaft or by its handle?

4. How does a wheel and axle make work easier when force is applied to the wheel?

UNIT PROJECT LINK

The ancient Egyptians used some simple machines to help them move the pyramid blocks. Use wood blocks as model pyramid blocks. Design and build some simple machines to help you move the blocks across a flat surface and to raise them some distance above the surface.

Wheels Turning Wheels

When you hear the word *wheel*, what pictures spring into your mind? Pictures of cars, buses, bicycles, skateboards, and numerous other things that move from one place to another on wheels might come to mind.

But many wheels don't go anywhere! Instead, they stay in one place and help you do work. A doorknob is a wheel that doesn't go anywhere. So is the faucet on a sink. And a Ferris wheel is, of course, a wheel.

Double Your Wheels

Actually, all these devices are made of two wheels, one large and one small, connected to each other. The combination is called a wheel and axle.

A **wheel and axle** is a simple machine made up of two wheels that

The circle turned by the wrench is the wheel. What "axle" does the wheel turn? ▶

turn, or pivot, around the same point. Effort is usually applied to the larger wheel. This force causes the smaller resistance wheel, called the axle, to turn in the same direction.

Where Are the Wheels?

Does a wrench look like a wheel to you? With many wheel-and-axle systems, you have to imagine the wheel part. If you've ever tried to remove a nut from a bolt with your bare hands, you know that a wrench makes the job easier. The wrench turns in a circle, causing the smaller nut to turn also. The wrench handle acts as the wheel in a wheel-and-axle machine.

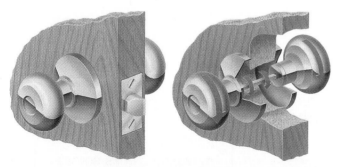

▲ The doorknob is the wheel; it turns the axle that runs through the door.

▲Turning the handle causes the axle to turn. Rope attached to a bucket winds around the axle, raising the bucket of water. With each turn, the effort force exerted on the handle travels much farther than the resistance, which is the bucket of water.

Now look at the picture above of the wheel and axle used to raise a bucket of water from a well. The effort force applied to the handle (wheel) is less than the force needed to raise the bucket directly. So a wheel and axle is another simple machine that makes work easier by reducing the amount of effort force that a person exerts to do work.

You could reduce your effort force still more by increasing the size of the wheel. Of course, as you increase the size of the large wheel, you have to turn it through a greater distance to raise the bucket. And this will take more time. So you lose speed as you reduce your effort force.

Speed's the Thing

What would happen if effort were applied to the smaller wheel of a wheel and axle? That's what happens in a Ferris wheel. A force is applied to the axle of the Ferris wheel, causing it to turn. Each time the axle moves through a short distance, the cars near the outer edge of the large wheel move through a much greater distance, and move much faster.

When effort is applied to the small wheel of a wheel and axle, distance—and speed—are gained. What's sacrificed? Force. A great effort force must be applied to the small wheel. Fortunately, in a Ferris wheel the effort force is supplied by an engine.

A wheel and axle is a simple machine. It helps make work easier. It is not the same as the wheels that spin *around* an axle. Those kinds of wheels only reduce friction. ■

▲ In a Ferris wheel, a large force is applied to the axle, causing the outer rim of the wheel to move at high speed.

Gearing Up

On an old-fashioned bicycle, the pedals are attached to the large front wheel. When the rider pushes on the pedals, the force exerted makes the large wheel turn. This is an example of a wheel and axle in which the effort force is applied to the smaller wheel. Recall that when a force is applied to the smaller wheel, the larger wheel moves a greater distance at a greater speed.

Today's bicyclists still apply force to a bike's pedals. However, the pedals of a modern bicycle are not connected to either of the bicycle's wheels. The pedals are connected to a gear. A gear is a wheel with teeth.

Transferring Force

Gears transfer force. In other words, a force applied to one gear is "sent" somewhere else, usually to another gear. In a bicycle the pedals are part of a wheel and axle, which is connected to a large gear. A chain connects this gear to a smaller gear, which is attached to the back wheel. When the pedals are turned, the front gear turns, moving the chain that turns the rear gear. When the rear gear turns, the back wheel turns—and off you go.

▲ **On a multispeed bicycle, the gearshift lever is used to switch the chain from one set of gears to another.**

When pedaling up a steep hill, a bicyclist shifts the chain to the larger rear gears. This shift makes it easier to pedal. You apply less force over a greater distance. When riding on level ground, the bicyclist shifts the chain to the smaller rear gears. This makes it harder to pedal, but it increases the distance the bicycle moves with each pedal stroke.

Does all of this sound complicated? It probably is, especially if you try to imagine all the gears working at once. However, if you think about one pair of gears at a time, it's much simpler. Fortunately, when you're out riding your bike, you don't have to think about how the gear system works. When you come to a hill, you just have to know when to shift. ■

Compound Machines

The ringing of your alarm clock announces that morning has arrived. You yawn, hardly noticing the rumble of a truck outside your window. You peek out and see three workers unloading a crate from a truck.

The crate holds a washing machine that your parents have ordered. You watch as the men deposit the crate at the foot of the stairs leading to your front door and then drive off. Suddenly you remember something your mother told you yesterday. The workers are not allowed to carry the crate up the steps and into the house. Your mother also told you it would be your job to find a way to get the crate into the house. Impossible! That crate must weigh more than you do.

Making the Job Easier

As you dress, you think of a possible solution. You remember that a simple machine makes a job easier. Perhaps you can use a simple machine to get the crate up the stairs.

To start, you lay a board against the stairs. The slanted board is an inclined plane. And you know that moving an object up an inclined plane is easier than lifting it. You try to push the crate up the board, but it won't budge. Even after you put rollers under the crate to reduce friction, you can only move it a few centimeters. Do you give up?

Machine Team

You try to think of other machines that might make the job easier. What

▲ A simple machine helps to make work easier.

▲ Sometimes one simple machine isn't enough to get the job done.

▲ When you combine simple machines, you also combine their mechanical advantages.

plane and a pulley system. By combining these machines you did a job you could not otherwise have done.

Each machine gave you an advantage; each multiplied your effort force on the crate. The combination of machines multiplied your effort enough to enable you to raise the crate to the top of the steps.

Compound Machines All Around You

Most of the machines that make life easier are compound machines. The truck that delivered the crate is a very complex compound machine. It's made up of wheel-and-axle systems, levers, and gears. Even your bicycle combines many simple machines.

Most compound machines used in and around a home are much simpler machines than a truck or a bicycle. Can openers are made up of at least two simple machines. How many simple machines make up the can opener in your home? Hint: Remember that a wedge is a kind of inclined plane.

Search your home for compound machines. Identify the simple machines that make up each of these compound machines. ■

about a lever? No, a lever won't work. How about a pulley? Pulleys can make work easier by reducing the effort you need to exert.

You set up a single, movable pulley system as shown. Then you stand at the top of the stairs and pull. Much to your surprise, the carton moves slowly but surely up the ramp. By combining a couple of simple machines—a ramp and a pulley—you have accomplished a task that you thought was impossible.

Multiplying Forces

Do you realize that you have built a compound machine? A **compound machine** is a machine that's made up of two or more simple machines. Your compound machine is made up of two kinds of simple machines—an inclined

---

INVESTIGATION 3

1. Explain why a water faucet is a type of wheel-and-axle machine.

2. Using a short screwdriver that has a thin handle, you try unsuccessfully to remove a screw from a board. Would you try using a screwdriver with a thicker handle or a screwdriver with a longer shaft? Explain your answer.

REFLECT & EVALUATE

WORD POWER

fulcrum   lever
machine   pulley
compound machine
inclined plane
mechanical advantage
wheel and axle

👤 On Your Own
Review the terms in the list. Then use as many terms as you can in a paragraph about simple machines.

👥 With a Partner
Mix up the letters of each term in the list. Provide a clue for each term and challenge your partner to unscramble the letters and name each term.

BUILD YOUR PORTFOLIO

Make a chart that describes four types of simple machines, explains how each makes work easier, and shows common examples. Use pictures cut from magazines or your own drawings to illustrate the chart.

Analyze Information
Identify the type of simple machine shown in each diagram. Then explain how each machine makes work easier.

A   B   C

Assess Performance
Design an experiment to determine how the distance between the threads of two different screws affects the amount of force needed to drive the screw into wood. Use screws of the same length but different numbers of threads, a piece of wood, and a screwdriver. Relate your observations to the formula for finding the mechanical advantage of an inclined plane.

Problem Solving

1. Patricia wants to use an inclined plane to move a large box onto a platform 2 m above the ground. She has two boards—one is 4 m long and the other is 6 m long. Which board will provide the greater mechanical advantage if used as a ramp up to the platform? Explain.

2. A shovel is an example of a lever. Decide whether a shovel is a first-class, second-class, or third-class lever, and explain your reasoning.

3. Imagine you work at a construction site. You want to move a roll of roofing paper to the roof of the building you are working on. Will the job be easier using a single fixed pulley or a single movable pulley? Explain.

Throughout this unit you've investigated questions related to energy, work, and machines. How will you use what you've learned and share that information with others? Here are some ideas.

Hold a Big Event
to Share Your Unit Project

After you have designed machines to help you move large wooden blocks, use them to build a pyramid. Better yet, work with a group to design your own building or structure. Draw up plans and show them to your teacher for approval. Then use your machines to build it. Invite your parents and friends to visit your classroom to view the machines your group has made and to learn about how ancient Egyptians might have used similar devices in building the Great Pyramid at Giza.

Experiment

Plan a long-term project based on an activity in this unit. You might want to build a scale model of a real roller coaster or a compound machine that combines all the different simple machines. Set up a plan for your experiment and show it to your teacher before you begin.

Research

Read one of the books mentioned in this unit. You might want to learn about what life was like on a farm years ago and compare the machines used then with the types of machinery used on a modern farm.

Take Action

Did you design a new, breathtaking roller coaster ride? Did you figure out how a simple machine can make some task at school or home a little easier? Choose one of these ideas or develop one of your own and take action. Share your information with others.

SCIENCE Handbook

THINK LIKE A SCIENTIST

You don't have to be a professional scientist to act and think like one. Thinking like a scientist mostly means using common sense. It also means learning how to test your ideas in a careful way.

In other words, *you* can think like a scientist.

Make a Hypothesis

Plan and Do a Test

Make Observations

To think like a scientist, you should learn as much as you can by observing things around you. Everything you hear and see is a clue about how the natural world works.

Ask a Question

Look for patterns. You'll get ideas and ask questions like these:

- Do all birds eat the same seeds?

- How does the time that the Sun sets change from day to day?

Make a Guess Called a Hypothesis

If you have an idea about why or how something happens, make an educated guess, or *hypothesis*, that you can test. For example, let's suppose that your hypothesis about the sunset time is that it changes by one minute each day.

Plan and Do a Test

Plan how to test your hypothesis. Your plan would need to consider some of these problems:

- How will you measure the time that the Sun sets?

- Will you measure the time every day?

- For how many days or weeks do you need to measure?

Record and Analyze What Happens

When you test your idea, you need to observe carefully and write down, or record, everything that happens. When you finish collecting data, you may need to do some calculations with it. For example, you might want to calculate how much the sunset time changes in a week or a month.

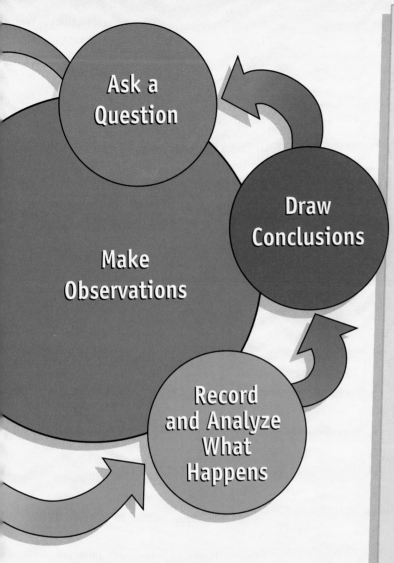

Ask a
Question

Draw
Conclusions

Make
Observations

Record
and Analyze
What
Happens

Draw Conclusions

Whatever happens in a test, think about all the reasons for your results. For example, you might wonder what causes the time of sunset to change. You might also ask when the earliest and latest sunsets occur during the year. Sometimes this thinking leads to a new hypothesis.

If the time of the sunset changes by one minute each day, think about what else the data shows you. Can you predict the time that the Sun will set one month from now?

PRACTICE SCIENTIFIC REASONING SKILLS

To think like a scientist, you need to practice certain ways of thinking.

Always check for yourself.
Always ask, "How do I really know it's true?" Be willing to find out for yourself.

Be honest and careful about what you observe.
It's easy to only look for the results you expect. It's harder to see the unexpected. But unexpected results lead scientists to ask more questions. They also provide information on how things work.

Don't be afraid to be wrong.
Based on their observations, scientists make many hypotheses. Not all of these hypotheses turn out to be correct. But scientists can learn from wrong "guesses," because even wrong guesses result in information that leads to knowledge.

Keep an open mind about possible explanations.
Make sure to think about all the reasons why something might have happened. Consider all the explanations that you can think of.

WHAT CAUSES THE ROCK IN STATUES TO WEAR AWAY?

Make Observations

Ask a Question

Donelle and Ramon were walking through downtown when Ramon pointed to a statue, laughed, and said, "Look, that poor guy's nose has fallen off." Donelle laughed and as they both took a closer look at the statue, they could see that most of the statue's face was missing. Even the statue's body was pitted.

Donelle thought she knew why. She suspected that rain, snow, and ice were destroying the statue. "But it's stone," Ramon argued. "Stone doesn't dissolve in water. Does it?" "But don't we get acid rain here?" Donelle replied. "Maybe acid rain destroys stone."

The next day in school, Donelle described the "melting" statue to the class. Mr. Reynolds, their teacher, suggested that the class set up an experiment to find out what might be causing the damage to the statue. To begin, they came up with some questions that they wanted to answer.

What is destroying this statue?

Is rain destroying this statue?

Are cold winter temperatures destroying this statue?

The class decided that the first question was not specific enough. They

> Here's an example of an everyday problem and how thinking like a scientist can help you explore it.

Make a Hypothesis

Make Observations

Before the class could begin setting up an experiment, there were some things they had to find out about the problem. First, they had to find out what the statue was made of. Ramon contacted City Hall and found out that the statue was made out of a stone called limestone.

Donelle told her classmates that she thought that the rain that fell on their town was sometimes acid. So Donelle and her classmates took samples of rainwater. They tested the rainwater with litmus paper and discovered that the rain was acidic.

The class thought about the new information they now had. It was time to use this information to formulate a hypothesis that they could test. Their hypothesis was "Acid rain eats away limestone."

decided to test whether rain could be destroying the statue. Students were curious about whether pollution in the air, and thus in the rain, might be affecting the statue.

Scientific investigations usually begin with something that you have noticed or read about. As you think about what you already know, you'll discover some ideas that you're not sure about. This will help you to ask the question that you really want to answer.

When you use what you have observed to suggest a possible answer to your question, you are making a *hypothesis*. Be sure that your hypothesis is an idea that you can test somehow. If you can't think of an experiment or a model to test your hypothesis, try changing it. Sometimes it's better to make a simpler, clearer hypothesis that answers only part of your question.

Make Observations

Plan and Do a Test

Ramon, Donelle, and their classmates designed a way to test their hypothesis. First, Mr. Reynolds got some fairly equal-sized lumps of limestone for the class to use. Donelle set up three flat-bottomed beakers big enough to hold the chunks of limestone. Ramon created a table for recording information.

The students had discussed what kind of solutions they should use in each beaker. They decided to put rainwater they'd collected in one beaker. They decided to put a more acidic solution in the second beaker. Mr. Reynolds provided them with a solution of weak sulfuric acid. The students knew that the third beaker should contain only pure, distilled water.

The third beaker served as the students' control. The control part of an experiment is almost identical to the other parts of the experiment. It is different in just one way: it doesn't have the condition that is being tested. In this case, the class was testing the effects on limestone of water that is acidic. To make sure that their results only reflect the effects of acid, and not something else that might be in water, the students set up a control in which acid was missing.

After the three beakers were each filled with their specific liquid and labeled, the students found the mass of each chunk of limestone and then put one in each beaker.

The students placed the beakers on a lab table at the back of the classroom. A square piece of glass was placed over each beaker to keep out dirt and dust that might affect the results.

One way to try out your hypothesis is to use a test called an experiment. When you plan an experiment, be sure that it helps you to answer your question. But even when you plan, things can happen that make the experiment confusing or make it not work properly. If this happens, you can change the plan or the experiment, and try again.

Make Observations

Record and Analyze What Happened

After seven days, the mass of each limestone chunk was found again. The mass was recorded on the chart on the board. The chunk was replaced in the same beaker. This was repeated every seven days.

The students recorded the mass of the limestone chunks for fourteen weeks. At the end of the experiment, their chart looked like the one on the next page.

The students analyzed the data on their chart. Donelle noted that the more acidic the solution in the beaker, the more mass the limestone "lost." Ramon noted that the mass of the limestone in the beaker containing distilled water remained the same. The limestone in the rainwater beaker "lost" some mass, but not as much as the limestone chunk in the beaker containing sulfuric acid.

Mass of Limestone Each Week (in grams)

	Week													
	1	**2**	**3**	**4**	**5**	**6**	**7**	**8**	**9**	**10**	**11**	**12**	**13**	**14**
Rainwater	83	83	82	82	81	80	80	79	79	78	77	77	76	75
Sulfuric acid solution	76	74	71	69	68	65	63	60	59	55	53	50	48	45
Distilled water	79	79	79	79	79	79	79	79	79	79	79	79	79	79

When you do an experiment, you need to write down, or record, your observations. Some of your observations might be numbers of things that you counted or measured. Your recorded observations are called data. When you record your data, you need to organize it in a way that helps you to understand it. Graphs and tables are helpful ways to organize data. Then think about the information you have collected. Analyze what it tells you.

Draw Conclusions

Make Observations

Both Ramon and Donelle thought that it looked like their hypothesis was supported. Water containing an acid, or acid rain, did eat away limestone. But Ramon was still not completely satisfied. He wondered if acid rain affected all kinds of stone in the same way, or if it destroyed only limestone. Ramon posed his question to Mr. Reynolds and the other students. Then Patrick added, "And I wonder if cold weather makes the effects of acid rain even worse."

It was soon evident that though their experiment had showed that acid rain does affect limestone, a whole new set of questions occurred to them.

After you have analyzed your data, you should use what you have learned to draw a conclusion. A conclusion is a statement that sums up what you learned. The conclusion should be about the question you asked. Think about whether the information you have gathered supports your hypothesis or not. If it does, figure out how to test out your idea more thoroughly. Also think about new questions you can ask.

SAFETY

The best way to be safe in the classroom is to use common sense. Prepare yourself for each activity before you start it. Get help from your teacher when there is a problem. Most important of all, pay attention. Here are some other ways that you can stay safe.

Stay Safe From Stains

- Wear protective clothing or an old shirt when you work with messy materials.
- If anything spills, wipe it up or ask your teacher to help you clean it up.

Stay Safe From Flames

- Keep your clothes away from open flames. If you have long or baggy sleeves, roll them up.
- Don't let your hair get close to a flame. If you have long hair, tie it back.

Stay Safe From Injuries

- Protect your eyes by wearing safety goggles when you are told that you need them.
- Keep your hands dry around electricity. Water is a good conductor of electricity, so you can get a shock more easily if your hands are wet.
- Be careful with sharp objects. If you have to press on them, keep the sharp side away from you.
- Cover any cuts you have that are exposed. If you spill something on a cut, be sure to wash it off immediately.
- Don't eat or drink anything unless your teacher tells you that it's okay.

Stay Safe During Cleanup

- Wash up after you finish working.
- Dispose of things in the way that your teachers tells you to.

MOST IMPORTANTLY

If you ever hurt yourself or one of your group members gets hurt, tell your teacher right away.

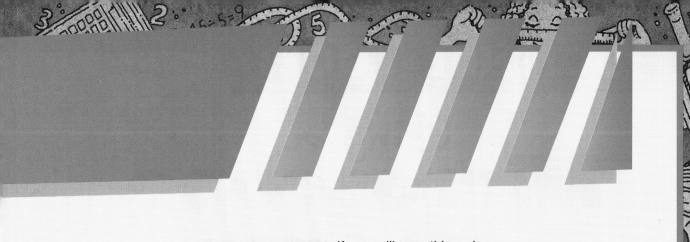

DON'T MAKE A MESS If you spill something, clean it up right away. When finished with an activity, clean up your work area. Dispose of things in the way your teacher tells you to.

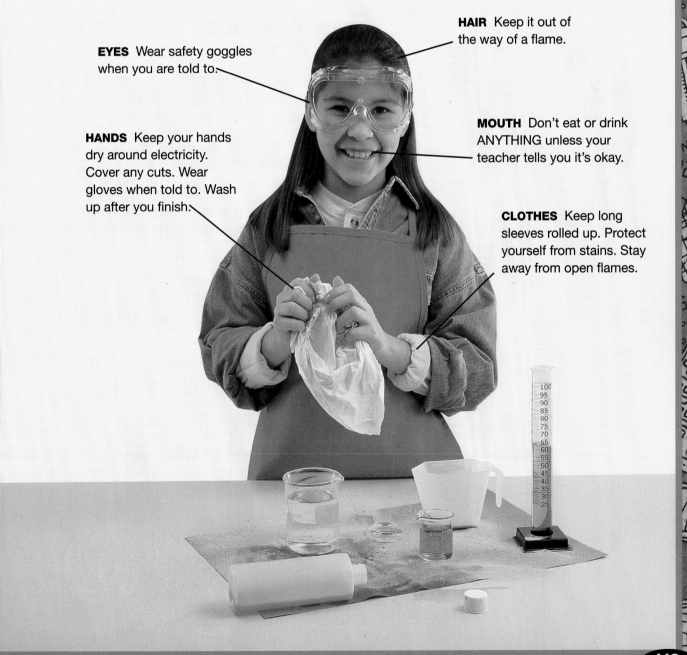

HAIR Keep it out of the way of a flame.

EYES Wear safety goggles when you are told to.

MOUTH Don't eat or drink ANYTHING unless your teacher tells you it's okay.

HANDS Keep your hands dry around electricity. Cover any cuts. Wear gloves when told to. Wash up after you finish.

CLOTHES Keep long sleeves rolled up. Protect yourself from stains. Stay away from open flames.

Using a Microscope

A microscope makes it possible to see very small things by magnifying them. Some microscopes have a set of lenses to magnify objects different amounts.

Examine Some Salt Grains

Handle a microscope carefully; it can break easily. Carry it firmly with both hands and avoid touching the lenses.

1. Turn the mirror toward a source of light. **NEVER** use the Sun as a light source.

2. Place a few grains of salt on the slide. Put the slide on the stage of the microscope.

3. While looking through the eyepiece, turn the adjustment knob on the back of the microscope to bring the salt grains into focus.

4. Raise the eyepiece tube to increase the magnification; lower it to decrease magnification.

Using a Calculator

After you've made measurements, a calculator can help you analyze your data. Some calculators have a memory key that allows you to save the result of one calculation while you do another.

Find an Average

The table shows the amount of rain that was collected using a rain gauge in each month of one year. You can use a calculator to help you find the average monthly rainfall.

1. Add the numbers. When you add a series of numbers, you don't need to press the equal sign until the last number is entered. Just press the plus sign after you enter each number (except the last one).

2. If you make a mistake while you are entering numbers, try to erase your mistake by pushing the clear entry (CE) key or the clear (C) key. Then you can continue entering the rest of the numbers you are adding. If you can't fix your mistake, you can push the (C) key once or twice until the screen shows 0. Then start over.

3. Your total should be 1,131. You can use the total to find the average. Just divide by the number of months in the year.

Rainfall	
Month	Rain (mm)
Jan.	214
Feb.	138
Mar.	98
Apr.	157
May	84
June	41
July	5
Aug.	23
Sept.	48
Oct.	75
Nov.	140
Dec.	108

These keys run the calculator's memory functions.

This key erases the last entry.

Using a Balance

A balance is used to measure mass. Mass is the amount of matter in an object. Place the object to be massed in the left pan. Place standard masses in the right pan.

Measure the Mass of an Orange

1. Check that the empty pans are balanced, or level with each other. The pointer at the base should be on the middle mark. If it needs to be adjusted, move the slider on the back of the balance a little to the left or right.

2. Place an orange on the left pan. Notice that the pointer moves and that the pans are no longer level with each other. Then add standard masses, one at a time, to the right pan. When the pointer is at the middle mark again, the pans are balanced. Each pan holds the same amount of mass.

3. Each standard mass is marked to show the number of grams it contains. Add the number of grams marked on the masses in the pan. The total is the mass in grams of the orange.

Using a Spring Scale

A spring scale is used to measure force. You can use a spring scale to find the weight of an object in newtons. You can also use the scale to measure other forces.

Measure the Weight of an Object

1. Place the object in a net bag, and hang it from the hook on the bottom of the spring scale. Or, if possible, hang the object directly from the hook.

2. Slowly lift the scale by the top hook. Be sure the object to be weighed continues to hang from the bottom hook.

3. Wait until the pointer on the face of the spring scale has stopped moving. Read the number next to the pointer to determine the weight of the object in newtons.

Measure Friction

1. Hook the object to the bottom of the spring scale. Use a rubber band to connect the spring scale and object if needed.

2. Gently pull the top hook of the scale parallel to the floor. When the object starts to move, read the number of newtons next to the pointer on the scale. This number is the force of friction between the floor and the object as you drag the object.

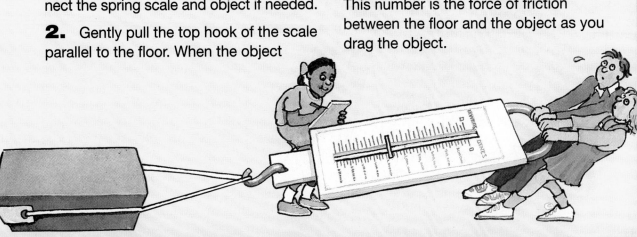

Using a
Thermometer

A thermometer is used to measure temperature. When the liquid in the tube of a thermometer gets warmer, it expands and moves farther up the tube. Different units can be used to measure temperature, but scientists usually use the Celsius scale.

Measure the Temperature of a Cold Liquid

1. Half-fill a cup with chilled liquid.

2. Hold the thermometer so that the bulb is in the center of the liquid.

3. Wait until you see the liquid in the tube stop moving. Read the scale line that is closest to the top of the liquid in the tube.

Measuring
Volume

A graduated cylinder, a measuring cup, and a beaker are used to measure volume. Volume is the amount of space something takes up. Most of the containers that scientists use to measure volume have a scale marked in milliliters (mL).

Measure the Volume of Juice

1. Pour the juice into a measuring container.

2. Move your head so that your eyes are level with the top of the juice. Read the scale line that is closest to the surface of the juice. If the surface of the juice is curved up on the sides, look at the lowest point of the curve.

3. You can estimate the value between two lines on the scale to obtain a more accurate measurement.

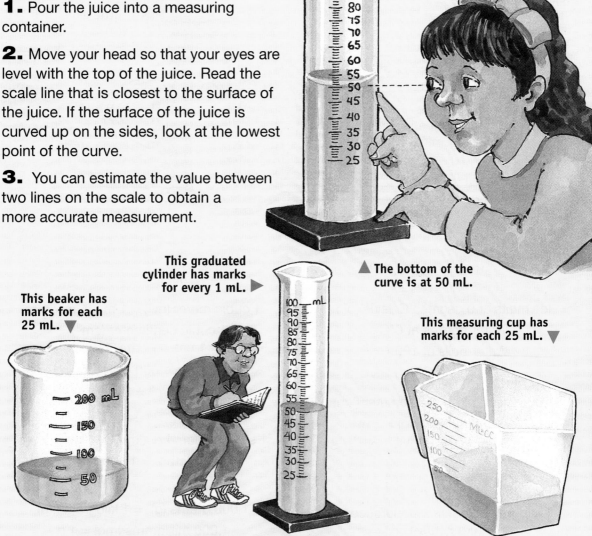

▲ The bottom of the curve is at 50 mL.

This graduated cylinder has marks for every 1 mL. ▶

This beaker has marks for each 25 mL. ▼

This measuring cup has marks for each 25 mL. ▼

Each container above has 50 mL of juice.

MEASUR

Area
A basketball court covers about 4,700 ft². It covers about 435 m².

Volume
1 L of sports drink is a little more than 1 qt.

Temperature
The temperature at an indoor basketball game might be 25°C, which is 77°F.

SI Measures

Temperature
Ice melts at 0 degrees Celsius (°C)

Water freezes at 0°C

Water boils at 100°C

Length and Distance
1,000 meters (m) = 1 kilometer (km)

100 centimeters (cm) = 1 m

10 millimeters (mm) = 1 cm

Force
1 newton (N) =
1 kilogram x meter/second/second
(kg x m/s²)

Volume
1 cubic meter (m³) = 1 m x 1 m x 1 m

1 cubic centimeter (cm³) =
1 cm x 1 cm x 1 cm

1 liter (L) = 1,000 milliliters (mL)

1 cm³ = 1 mL

Area
1 square kilometer (km²) = 1 km x 1 km

1 hectare = 10,000 m²

Mass
1,000 grams (g) = 1 kilogram (kg)

1,000 milligrams (mg) = 1 g

EMENTS

Mass and Weight
A basketball has a mass of about 650 g.
It weighs about $1\frac{1}{2}$ lb.

**Length/
Distance**
A basketball rim is about
10 ft high, or a little more
than 3 m from the floor.

Rates (SI and English)

km/h = kilometers per hour

m/s = meters per second

mph = miles per hour

English Measures

Volume of Fluids

8 fluid ounces (fl oz) = 1 cup (c)

2 c = 1 pint (pt)

2 pt = 1 quart (qt)

4 qt = 1 gallon (gal)

Temperature

Ice melts at 32 degrees
Fahrenheit (°F)

Water freezes at 32°F

Water boils at 212°F

Length and Distance

12 inches (in.) = 1 foot (ft)

3 ft = 1 yard (yd)

5,280 ft = 1 mile (mi)

Weight

16 ounces (oz) = 1 pound (lb)   2,000 pounds = 1 ton (T)

GLOSSARY

Pronunciation Key

Symbol	Key Words
a	cat
ā	ape
ä	cot, car
e	ten, berry
ē	me
i	fit, here
ī	ice, fire
ō	go
ô	fall, for
oi	oil
o͝o	look, pull
o͞o	tool, rule
ou	out, crowd
u	up
ʉ	fur, shirt
ə	a in ago
	e in agent
	i in pencil
	o in atom
	u in circus
b	bed
d	dog
f	fall

Symbol	Key Words
g	get
h	help
j	jump
k	kiss, call
l	leg
m	meat
n	nose
p	put
r	red
s	see
t	top
v	vat
w	wish
y	yard
z	zebra
ch	chin, arch
ŋ	ring, drink
sh	she, push
th	thin, truth
th	then, father
zh	measure

A heavy stress mark ' is placed after a syllable that gets a heavy, or primary, stress, as in **picture** (pik'chər).

absolute age The actual age of an object. (E79) The *absolute age* of this statue is 3,500 years.

absolute magnitude The measure of a star's brightness, based on the amount of light it actually gives off. (B61) The Sun's *absolute magnitude* is less than that of many stars, but its *apparent magnitude* exceeds that of any other star.

adaptation (ad əp tā′shən) A structure or behavior that enables an organism to survive in its environment. (A70, A86) The thick fur of some animals is an *adaptation* to cold environments.

addiction (ə dik′shən) A condition in which a person has extreme difficulty in stopping the use of a drug. (G51) Sometimes it takes only a short time to develop an *addiction* to a drug.

alcohol (al′kə hôl) A drug that is found in some beverages, such as beer and wine. (G50) If a person drinks *alcohol* to excess, problems can occur.

alcoholism (al′kə hôl iz əm) A disease that results from the continual misuse of alcohol. (G60) Doctors continue to learn more about *alcoholism*.

amplitude (am′plə tood) A measure of the amount of energy in a sound wave. (F57) The *amplitude* of a loud sound is greater than the amplitude of a soft sound.

anticline (an′ti klīn) An upward fold of rock layers. (E84) Bending layers of rock formed an *anticline*.

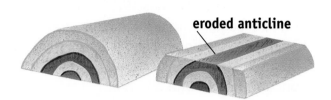

eroded anticline

apparent magnitude The measure of a star's brightness as seen from Earth. (B61) A star's *apparent magnitude* depends on the amount of light it gives off and on its distance from Earth.

asexual reproduction (ā sek′shoo əl rē prə duk′shən) A process in which offspring are produced from one or more cells of a single parent. (A62) In *asexual reproduction*, the offspring is identical to the parent.

audiocassette (ô′dē ō kə set) A small container holding magnetic tape that is used for playing or recording sound. (F92) We inserted an *audiocassette* into the tape recorder.

auditory nerve (ô′də tôr ē nʉrv) A nerve in the ear that carries nerve impulses to the brain. (G39, F85) The *auditory nerve* contains sensory neurons.

axis The imaginary line on which an object rotates. (B13) Earth's *axis* runs between the North and South poles.

B

Big Bang Theory A hypothesis, supported by data, that describes how the universe began with a huge explosion. (B39) The *Big Bang Theory* holds that everything in the universe was once concentrated at one tiny point.

biodiversity (bī ō də vʉr′sə tē) The variety of organisms that live in Earth's many ecosystems; the variety of plants and animals that live within a particular ecosystem. (D58) The *biodiversity* of an ecosystem quickly changes after a natural disaster.

biome (bī′ōm) A major land ecosystem having a distinct combination of plants and animals. (D48) Some *biomes*, such as the tundra, do not easily support human populations.

biosphere (bī′ō sfir) A self-sustaining natural system of living things and their environment. (B87) For humans to survive in space, they must bring along a version of their *biosphere.*

black dwarf The cool, dark body that is the final stage in the life cycle of a low-mass star. (B66) When the Sun dies, it will become a *black dwarf.*

black hole An extremely dense, invisible object in space whose gravity is so great that not even light can escape it. (B67) Scientists think that the remains of a very massive star can collapse following a supernova explosion to form a *black hole.*

blood alcohol concentration A test that determines the level of alcohol in a person's blood. (G61) A police officer can easily find out if a driver is drunk by giving a *blood alcohol concentration* test.

bone The hard tissue that forms the skeleton. Also, one of the organs that makes up the skeleton. (G8) The human hand contains many small *bones.*

C

caffeine (ka fēn′) A drug that acts as a stimulant and is present in coffee, many teas, cocoa, and some soft drinks. (G50) Many people prefer to drink herbal teas that do not have *caffeine* in them.

carbon dioxide–oxygen cycle *See* oxygen–carbon dioxide cycle.

cardiac muscle (kär′dē ak mus′əl) Involuntary muscle tissue that makes up the heart. (G17) *Cardiac muscle* contracts rhythmically.

carnivore (kär′nə vôr) A consumer that eats only other animals. (D19, D30) Lions are *carnivores* that prey on zebras and other large plant eaters.

cartilage (kärt′ə′l ij) Tough, flexible tissue that is part of the skeleton. (G8) *Cartilage* helps protect bones as they move at joints.

cell The basic unit of structure of all living things. (A24) Even though plant *cells* can be different sizes, they still have many of the same structures.

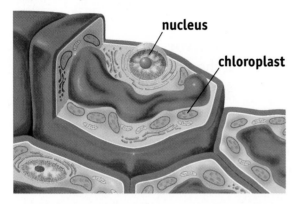

nucleus

chloroplast

cell membrane A thin layer that surrounds all cells and allows water and dissolved materials to pass into and out of the cell. (A24) In plant cells, the *cell membrane* lies inside the cell wall.

cell respiration The process of using oxygen to release energy from food. (A35, A45, D34) Animals and plants release carbon dioxide as a waste product of *cell respiration.*

cell wall The tough outer covering of a plant cell that gives the cell its rigid shape. (A24) A *cell wall* is not found in animal cells.

cementation (sē men tā′shən) A process in which minerals, deposited as water evaporates, bind sediments into solid rock. (E44) Sandstone is a sedimentary rock formed by *cementation.*

cerebellum (ser ə bel′əm) The second largest part of the brain, coordinating the body's muscles. (G32) The *cerebellum* allows smooth movement.

cerebrum (sə rē′brəm) The largest part of the brain in which the processes of thinking, learning, and reasoning take place. (G31) The *cerebrum* is the part of the brain that allows people to understand and remember ideas.

chloroplast (klôr′ə plast) A structure in plant cells that captures light energy that is used in the food-making process. (A33) *Chloroplasts* are located within cells in the leaves of a plant.

cleavage (klēv′ij) The tendency of some minerals to split along flat surfaces. (E15) Salt, or halite, shows *cleavage* in three planes.

clone (klōn) An exact copy of a parent organism produced by asexual reproduction. (A62) One way to *clone* a parent plant is to place a cutting from that plant in water.

coastal ocean A saltwater ecosystem that is relatively shallow and close to the shoreline and that supports an abundance of life. (D54) The *coastal ocean* is an ecosystem that lies beyond the shoreline.

comet (käm′it) A small object in space, made of ice, dust, gas, and rock, that orbits a star and that can form a gaseous tail. (B24) As a *comet* approaches the Sun, it begins to melt.

commensalism (kə men′səl iz əm)
A close relationship between two kinds
of organisms that benefits one of the
organisms while neither benefiting nor
hurting the other. (D21) The way that
some insects use their resemblance to
plants to hide from predators is an
example of *commensalism*.

community (kə myoo′nə tē) All the
organisms living together in a particular
ecosystem. (D10) Raccoons, deer, and
trees are part of a forest *community*.

compact disc (käm′pakt disk) A
small disk on which sounds are digitally
recorded and played back when read by
a laser beam. (F92) This *compact disc*,
or CD, contains one hour of music.

compound machine A machine that
is made up of two or more simple
machines. (C62) A pair of scissors is a
compound machine because it contains two kinds of simple machines—a
lever and a wedge.

compound microscope A viewing
instrument that uses two lenses to magnify objects many times. (F41) The
human hair appeared 1,000 times larger than actual size under the *compound
microscope*.

compression (kəm presh′ən) A
region in a sound wave where particles
have been pushed together. (F57) The
compressions produced by a vibrating
tuning fork are areas of greater than
normal air pressure.

concave lens (kän′kāv lenz) A lens
that is thicker at the edges than it is in
the middle and that causes light rays to
spread apart. (F32) A *concave lens* is
used to correct nearsightedness.

concave mirror A mirror that curves
inward at the middle. (F23) A *concave
mirror* is used in a reflecting telescope.

concrete (kän′krēt) A mixture of
rock material and cement that is used
as a building material. (E24) This sidewalk is made of *concrete*.

condensation (kän dən sā′shən)
The process by which water vapor is
changed to liquid water. (D36)
Condensation can occur on a glass
containing ice cubes.

conduction (kən duk′shən) The
transfer of heat energy by direct contact
between particles. (C13) Heat travels
through a metal by *conduction*.

conifer (kän′ə fər) A tree or shrub
that bears its seeds in cones. (A80) The
cones of each species of *conifer* are
distinct and different from each other.

constellation (kän stə lā′shən) A
group of stars that form a fixed pattern
in the night sky. (B10) The *constellation* Orion is best seen in the winter.

consumer (kən soom′ər) A living
thing that obtains energy by eating
other living things. (A36, D19) Meat
eaters and plant eaters are *consumers*.

contact lens A thin lens worn over the cornea of the eye, usually to correct vision problems. (F35) Some people use *contact lenses* rather than eyeglasses to improve their vision.

convection (kən vek′shən) The transfer of heat energy through liquids and gases by moving particles. (C13) Heat is carried throughout water in a pot on the stove by *convection*.

convex lens (kän′veks lenz) A lens that is thicker in the middle than at the edges and that brings light rays together. (F32) A *convex lens* is used to correct farsightedness.

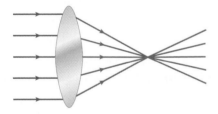

convex mirror A mirror that curves outward at the middle. (F23) The side-view mirror of a car is a *convex mirror*.

core The innermost layer of Earth, which consists of a molten outer part and a solid inner part. (E69) Temperatures inside the *core* of Earth are nearly as hot as those on the Sun's surface.

crest The highest point of a wave. (F57) The top of a water wave is its *crest*.

crust The outer layer of Earth. (E68) Earth's *crust* is a thin layer of rock.

cytoplasm (sīt′ō plaz əm) The jellylike substance that fills much of the cell. (A24) The nucleus, vacuoles, and many other cell structures float in the *cytoplasm*.

decibel (des′ə bəl) A unit used to measure the loudness or intensity of sound. (F79) Sounds that have an intensity greater than 120 *decibels* (db) can hurt your ears.

decomposer (dē kəm pōz′ər) A living thing that breaks down the remains of dead organisms. (A37, D19) *Decomposers*, such as bacteria, get their energy from the dead plants and animals they break down.

deciduous forest (dē sij′o͞o əs fôr′ist) A biome that contains many trees and in which rainfall is moderate. (D51) *Deciduous forests* support a great variety of animal life.

deforestation (dē fôr is tā′shən) A mass clearing of a forest. (A93) *Deforestation* is a major concern of environmentalists.

desert A biome in which plant life is not abundant and rainfall is low. (D50) Because *deserts* are dry, desert plants have adaptations to conserve water.

dicot (dī′kät) A flowering plant that produces seeds with two seed leaves, or food-storing leaves. (A81) A trait of a *dicot* is that its leaves have netlike veins.

drug A substance, other than food, that can affect the function of body cells and tissues and that produces a change in the body. (G50) A person sometimes takes a pain-killing *drug* after suffering a back injury.

ecosystem (ek'ō sis təm) An area in which living and nonliving things interact. (D10) An oak tree and the organisms that inhabit it can be thought of as a small *ecosystem.*

effort force The force that must be applied to an object to move the object. (C30) The tow truck applied enough *effort force* to pull the car away.

electromagnetic radiation (ē lek trō mag net'ik rā dē ā'shən) Wave energy given off by the Sun and some other objects. (F8) Visible light is a form of *electromagnetic radiation.*

electron microscope (ē lek'trän mī'krə skōp) A viewing instrument that magnifies objects thousands of times by using a beam of electrons instead of a beam of light. (F43) Doctors studied the virus through an *electron microscope.*

embryo (em'brē ō) An organism in its earliest stages of development; in most plants it is found inside a seed. (A61) When conditions for growth are suitable, the *embryo* inside the seed develops into a young plant.

endangered In danger of becoming extinct. (A92, D61) As the destruction of the Amazon rain forest continues, the number of *endangered* species increases.

energy The ability to do work or cause change. (C9, F8) *Energy* from the Sun warms the air.

erosion (ē rō'zhən) The wearing away and removing of rock and soil caused by such forces as wind and flowing water. (E84) The pounding waves caused *erosion* of the sandy shoreline.

Eustachian tube (yōō stā'kē ən tōōb) A tube that connects the throat and the middle ear. (F85) The *Eustachian tube* equalizes the air pressure on both sides of the eardrum.

evaporation (ē vap ə rā'shən) The process by which liquid water changes to water vapor. (D36) One phase of the water cycle is the *evaporation* of water from lakes, rivers, and oceans.

extinct (ek stiŋkt') No longer living as a species. (A92, D61) Traces of some *extinct* species can be found in fossils.

extraterrestrial (eks trə tə res'trē əl) A being from outer space; any object from beyond Earth. (B90) It would be extraordinary for scientists to discover that there is *extraterrestrial* life.

fault A break in rock along which rocks have moved. (E91) Forces within Earth's crust produce *faults*.

fern A nonseed plant that has roots, stems, and leaves and that is found mostly in moist, shady areas. (A79) On *ferns* that grow in tropical places, the fronds grow at the top of a tall trunk.

fertilization (fʉrt ′l ə zā′shən) The process by which a male sex cell joins with a female sex cell. In flowering plants, fertilization takes place in the pistil. (A60) *Fertilization* occurs after a pollen tube reaches the ovary.

filter A device that lets certain colors of light pass through while absorbing others. (F48) The stage manager placed a red *filter* over the spotlight.

flower The reproductive structure of a flowering plant. (A16) Petals protect the reproductive parts of a *flower*.

flowering plant Living organisms that reproduce by seeds formed in flowers and that have roots, stems, and leaves. (A81) *Flowering plants* are the most common group of plants on Earth today.

focal point The point at which light rays passing through a lens come together. (F32) Rays of light meet at the *focal point*.

fold A bend in a layer of rock. (E83) Forces within Earth can cause a *fold* to form in rock layers.

food chain The path of energy transfer from one living organism to another in an ecosystem. (A36, D29) Energy moves from producers to consumers in a *food chain*.

food web The overlapping food chains that link producers, consumers, and decomposers in an ecosystem. (A37, D30) Some consumers in a *food web* eat both plants and animals.

force A pull or a push. (C28) When you open a door, you apply a *force*.

fossil (fäs′əl) The remains or traces of a living thing from the past, preserved in rock. (E46, E77) *Fossils* can include imprints of animal skeletons pressed into rock.

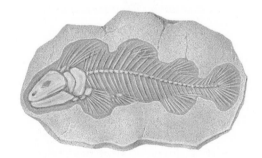

fracture (frak′chər) A break or crack in a bone. (G20) The skier suffered a leg *fracture* when he hit an icy patch.

free fall The motion of a freely falling object, such as a spacecraft in orbit around Earth. (B79) Astronauts experiencing *free fall* in space feel weightless.

frequency (frē′kwən sē) The number of waves (such as light or sound) produced in a unit of time, such as a second. (F18, F57) The *frequency* of light waves varies with the color of the light.

friction (frik′shən) Force produced by the rubbing of one thing against another; a force that acts to oppose motion. (C31) *Friction* prevents sneakers from slipping on a gym floor.

fruit The enlarged ovary of a flower that protects the developing seeds. (A61) Some *fruits*, such as peaches or mangoes, contain only one seed.

fulcrum (ful′krəm) The fixed point around which a lever pivots. (C50) If you use a lever to lift an object, the *fulcrum* is located between you and the object you are lifting.

galaxy (gal′ək sē) A vast group of billions of stars that are held together by gravity. (B70) The Milky Way is a typical spiral *galaxy*.

gas giant A large planet that is made up mostly of gaseous and liquid substances, with little or no solid surface. (B47) Jupiter is a *gas giant*.

geocentric model (jē ō sen′trik mäd′′l) A representation of the universe in which stars and planets revolve around Earth. (B37) Ptolemy proposed a *geocentric model* of the universe.

glucose (gloo′kōs) A sugar produced by plants that is the main source of energy for cells. (A33) *Glucose* is produced during photosynthesis.

grassland A biome containing many grasses but few trees and having low to moderate rainfall. (D50) Taller grasses occur in *grasslands* that have more abundant rainfall.

hardness A measure of how easily a mineral can be scratched. (E13) The *hardness* of diamond is greater than that of any other mineral.

hearing aid A small battery-powered electronic device that makes sounds louder. (F86) Most people who wear a *hearing aid* have improved hearing.

heliocentric model (hē lē ō sen′trik mäd′′l) A representation of the relationship between the Sun and planets in which the planets revolve around the Sun. (B37) Copernicus hypothesized a *heliocentric model* of the solar system.

herbivore (hʉr′bə vôr) A consumer that eats only plants or other producers. (D19, D30) Panda bears are *herbivores* that have a very limited diet because they only eat bamboo.

hertz (herts) A unit used to measure wave frequency. (F18, F68) If 100 waves are produced per second, the frequency of the wave is 100 *hertz.*

igneous rock (ig'nē əs räk) A type of rock that forms from melted rock that cools and hardens. (E40) *Igneous rock* forms from both magma and lava.

illegal drug A substance whose use is prohibited by law. (G50) One *illegal drug* in the United States is heroin.

inclined plane A simple machine with a sloping surface. It allows objects to be raised or lowered from one level to another without lifting them. (C43) A ramp is a kind of *inclined plane.*

index fossil (in'deks fäs'əl) A fossil used to determine the relative age of rock. (E78) The remains of a living thing that lived only at a certain time in the past makes a good *index fossil.*

information superhighway The futuristic concept of communications as an electronic highway system in which telephones, computers, and televisions are linked. (F93) The *information superhighway* will let students do library research from their homes.

intensity (in ten'sə tē) A measure of the amount of energy of sound. (F78) A sound that has high *intensity* is loud enough to be heard from a distance.

Internet (in'tər net) A system of interconnected computer networks. (F94) Telephone lines link computer users with the *Internet.*

joint The place where two bones meet. (G8) Your elbow *joint* enables you to bend your arm.

joule (jo͞ol) The basic unit of energy and of work. (C19) Scientists measure amounts of energy in *joules.*

kinetic energy The energy that something has because of its motion. (C20) As a boulder rolls down a steep hill, it gains *kinetic energy.*

lake A freshwater ecosystem characterized by still, or standing water. (D53) *Lakes* support fish, birds, algae, and other forms of life.

lava (lä'və) Melted rock material that reaches Earth's surface before it cools and hardens. (E41) A volcano carries *lava* to Earth's surface.

leaf A plant part in which photosynthesis takes place. (A14) In a plant such as cabbage, it is the *leaf* that people eat.

lens A piece of glass or other transparent material with at least one curved surface that brings together or spreads apart light rays passing through it. (F32) The *lens* in a camera focuses an image on the film.

lever (lev'ər) A simple machine made up of a bar that pivots around a fixed point (a fulcrum). (C50) A *lever* can help lift a heavy object with less effort.

ligament (lig'ə mənt) A band of strong tissue that connects bones and holds them in place. (G8) A *ligament* holds bones together at a joint.

light-year A unit of measurement representing the distance that light travels in one year. (B61) Scientists use the unit called a *light-year* when measuring the distances to stars.

luster (lus'tər) The way that the surface of a mineral looks when it reflects light. (E13) Silver and gold have a shiny, metallic *luster.*

machine A device that makes work easier by reducing the amount of force needed to do a job. (C43) A *machine* can make it easier to move, lift, carry, or cut something.

magma (mag'mə) Melted rock material that forms deep within Earth. (E40) Some igneous rocks, such as granite, form from *magma.*

mantle A thick layer of rock between the crust and the core of Earth. (E69) The top of the *mantle* is solid rock but below that is a section of rock that can flow.

mechanical advantage (mə kan'i-kəl ad vant'ij) The number of times that a machine multiplies the effort force applied to it. (C44) To find the *mechanical advantage* of an inclined plane, divide the length of its sloping surface by its height.

medulla (mi dul'ə) The part of the brain that controls the involuntary functions of the body, such as heart rate and breathing. (G32) The *medulla* is located in the brain stem and controls many things you do without thinking.

metamorphic rock (met ə môr'fik räk) A type of rock that forms from existing rocks because of changes caused by heat, pressure, or chemicals. (E47) Slate is a *metamorphic rock* that forms from the sedimentary rock shale.

meteor (mēt'ē ər) A piece of rock or metal from space that enters Earth's atmosphere. (B25) A *meteor* appears as a streak of light, which is why it is also called a shooting star.

meteorite (mēt'ē ər īt) The remaining material of a meteor that has landed on the ground. (B26) In 1902, scientists were able to examine the largest *meteorite* ever known to land in the United States.

Milky Way Galaxy A gigantic cluster of billions of stars that is home to our solar system. (B70) The Sun is located in one of the arms of the *Milky Way Galaxy*.

mineral A solid element or compound found in nature and having a definite chemical composition and crystal structure. (E12) Quartz is a *mineral*.

model Something used or made to represent an object or an idea. (E68) The plastic *model* airplane was a miniature copy of the actual airplane.

monocot (män′ō kät) A flowering plant that produces seeds with a single seed leaf, or food-storing leaf. (A81) About one third of all flowering plants are *monocots*.

moon A natural object that revolves around a planet. (B44) The planet Mars has two known *moons*.

moss A small nonseed plant that lacks roots, stems, and leaves and grows mostly in moist areas in woods or near stream banks. (A78) The leaflike part of *moss* only grows a few centimeters above ground.

motor neuron (mōt′ər nōō′rän) A nerve cell that carries impulses from the brain and spinal cord to muscles and glands in the body. (G28) When people exercise, *motor neurons* carry impulses from the spinal cord to different muscles in the body.

mutualism (myōō′chōō əl iz əm) A close relationship between two or more organisms in which all organisms benefit. (D22) Bees carrying pollen from flower to flower as they obtain nectar is an example of *mutualism*.

narcotic (när kät′ik) A habit-forming drug that depresses the function of the nervous system. (G55) Morphine is a *narcotic* drug that is often given to cancer patients.

nebula (neb′yə lə) A huge cloud of gas and dust found in space. (B64) A *nebula* can form when a supernova explodes.

nerve impulse (nʉrv im′puls) A message carried through the body by neurons. (G28) *Nerve impulses* pass from one neuron to another as they move through the body.

neuron (nōō′rän) A nerve cell. (G28) The brain is connected to all parts of the body by *neurons*.

neutron star (nōō′trän stär) The remains of a massive star that has exploded in a supernova. (B67) A typical *neutron star* is less than 20 km in diameter.

newton A unit used to measure force. (C29) About 300 *newtons* of force was applied in moving the rock.

nicotine (nik′ə tēn) A drug found in the tobacco plant. (G50) People become addicted to cigarettes because of the *nicotine* in the tobacco.

nitrogen cycle The cycle through which nitrogen gas is changed into compounds that can be used by living things and then is returned to the atmosphere. (D42) The *nitrogen cycle* is of great importance to all life forms because nitrogen is needed to make protein.

noise pollution The occurrence of loud or unpleasant sound in the environment. (F80) The sounds of city traffic are a form of *noise pollution.*

nonseed plant A plant that reproduces without forming seeds. (A78) Mosses are *nonseed plants.*

nucleus (nōō′klē əs) The cell structure that controls all of a cell's activities. (A24) The *nucleus* was clearly visible after it was stained.

octave (äk′tiv) The series of eight notes that makes up a musical scale. (F69) The music student practiced playing *octaves* on the piano.

omnivore (äm′ni vôr) A consumer that eats both plants and animals. (D19, D30) Because they eat both meats and vegetables, many humans are *omnivores.*

opaque (ō pāk′) Not letting light through. (F47) The *opaque* curtains kept out the sunlight.

open ocean A large saltwater ecosystem containing both floating and free-swimming organisms. (D55) The *open ocean* covers much of Earth's surface.

optic nerve A bundle of neurons that carries impulses from the eye to the brain. (G39) If there is damage to the *optic nerve,* messages from the eye cannot be received by the brain.

ore (ôr) A mineral or rock that contains enough of a metal to making mining the metal profitable. (E27) Hemalite is an *ore* mined for its iron content.

overtone A fainter, higher tone that harmonizes with the main tone produced by a musical instrument or the human voice. (F58) The blending of *overtones* gives the flute its unique sound.

oxygen–carbon dioxide cycle A natural cycle in which plants and other producers use carbon dioxide and produce oxygen, and living things use oxygen and produce carbon dioxide. (B86, D34) The *oxygen–carbon dioxide cycle* must be duplicated in space if humans wish to make long voyages to other planets.

— P —

parasitism (par'ə sīt iz əm) A relationship between two organisms in which one organism lives on or in the other, feeds upon it, and usually harms it. (D21) The way in which fleas live off dogs is an example of *parasitism.*

phloem cell (flō'əm sel) A plant cell that, when linked with other similar cells, forms a system of tubes for carrying nutrients from the leaves down through the stem and root. (A11) The *phloem cells* form a major transport system in plants.

phonograph (fō'nə graf) A device that reproduces sounds recorded on a disk. (F90) We played old records on the *phonograph.*

photosynthesis (fōt ō sin'thə sis) The process by which producers, such as plants, make their own food by using energy from the Sun. (A33) *Photosynthesis* takes place primarily in the leaves of plants.

pistil (pis'til) The female reproductive structure of a flower. (A16) A *pistil* consists of three main parts—the stigma, the style, and the ovary.

pitch The highness or lowness of a sound. (F68) A tuba produces sounds with a low *pitch.*

plane mirror A mirror that has a flat surface. (F23) The mirror over the bathroom sink is a *plane mirror.*

planet A large body in space that orbits a star and does not produce light on its own. (B17) Earth is one of nine known *planets* that revolve around the Sun.

plant kingdom A major group of living things that are multicellular and that carry out photosynthesis. (A78) Living organisms in the *plant kingdom* make their own food.

pollination (päl ə nā'shən) The transfer of pollen from the male part of one flower to the female part of another flower. (A60) Some *pollination* is done by insects.

population (päp yoo lā'shən) A group of the same kind of organisms that live in an area. (D10) There is a huge *population* of frogs in that marsh.

potential energy The energy that an object has because of its position or structure; stored energy. (C18) A coiled spring has *potential energy.*

precipitation (prē sip ə tā'shən) The process by which water from clouds falls back to the Earth. (D36) *Precipitation* falls to the Earth in the form of rain or snow.

producer (prō d$\overline{oo}$s'ər) An organism that makes its own food through photosynthesis. (A36, D18) Plants and algae are examples of *producers*.

protein (prō'tēn) Organic compounds that form the structure and control the processes that take place in living things. (D41) *Proteins* provide the body with materials that help cells grow and repair themselves.

protostar (prōt'ō stär) A concentration of matter found in space that is the beginning of a star. (B64) When the temperature inside a *protostar* becomes high enough, nuclear reactions begin and it turns into a star.

pulley (p$\overline{oo}$l'ē) A simple machine made up of a wheel around which a rope or chain is passed. (C53) A *pulley* helps lift objects that would be too heavy to lift directly.

quarry (kwôr'ē) A mine, usually near or at Earth's surface, from which rock is removed. (E52) Granite, sandstone, limestone, slate, and marble are some rocks that come from a *quarry*.

radiation (rā dē ā'shən) The transfer of energy by waves. (C11) Energy given off by the Sun travels as *radiation* through space.

radio telescope A gigantic antenna designed to receive radio signals from space. (B92) *Radio telescopes* are important tools for studying distant stars and galaxies.

rarefaction (rer ə fak'shən) A region in a sound wave where there are fewer particles than normal. (F57) The *rarefactions* that a vibrating violin string produces are areas of lower than normal air pressure.

receptor (ri sep'tər) A sensory neuron that receives stimuli from the environment. (G37) Sensory *receptors* in the skin make it possible for people to feel heat, cold, pressure, touch, and pain.

red giant A very large old reddish star that has greatly expanded and cooled as its fuel has begun to run out. (B65) As the Sun reaches old age, it will turn into a *red giant*.

reflecting telescope An instrument for viewing distant objects that uses a curved mirror at the back of its tube to gather light and produce an image. (B22, F39) This observatory uses a *reflecting telescope* to observe faraway galaxies.

reflection (ri flek′shən) The bouncing of light or sound off a surface. (F22) The *reflection* of sunlight off the snow made us squint.

reflex (rē′fleks) A simple behavior pattern involving an automatic response to a stimulus. (G42) The girl's automatic *reflex* quickly got her foot out of the hot water.

refracting telescope An instrument for viewing distant objects that uses two lenses to gather light and produce an image. (B21) The *refracting telescope* gave us a closer look at the Moon.

refraction (ri frak′shən) The bending of light as it passes from one material into another. (F24) Light traveling from air into water will undergo *refraction*.

relative age The age of an object as compared to other objects. (E78) The order of layers of rock shows the *relative ages* of the layers.

resistance force A force that resists, or opposes, motion. (C30) Friction is a *resistance force*.

retina (ret′′n ə) The light-sensitive area at the back of the eye on which an image is formed. (F34) The *retina* contains two kinds of cells.

revolution (rev ə loo′shən) The movement of an object around another object or point. (B14) It takes about 365 days for Earth to make one *revolution* around the Sun.

river A freshwater ecosystem characterized by running water. (D52) Salmon are able to swim against the current in a *river*.

rock The solid material composed of minerals that forms Earth's crust. Also, the material, sometimes molten, that forms Earth's inner layers. (E40) *Rocks* are weathered by wind and rain.

rock cycle The continuous series of changes that rocks undergo. (E60) In the *rock cycle*, changes are brought about by factors such as weathering, melting, cooling, or pressure.

root The underground part of a plant that anchors the plant and absorbs water and nutrients. (A10) Carrots and turnips have only one large single *root*.

rotation (rō tā′shən) The spinning motion of an object on its axis. (B14) It takes about 24 hours for Earth to make one complete *rotation*.

— S —

sapling (sap′liŋ) A young tree. (A67) The year after a tree seed germinates, the young plant is called a *sapling*.

satellite (sat′′l īt) A natural or human-built object that revolves around another object in space. (B44) The Moon is a natural *satellite* of Earth.

sediment (sed'ə mənt) Bits of weathered rocks and minerals and pieces of dead plants or animals. (E43) Over time, *sediments* can form sedimentary rocks, such as sandstone and limestone.

sedimentary rock (sed ə men'tər ē räk) A type of rock that forms when sediments harden. (E43) Most *sedimentary rocks* form in layers.

seed coat A tough, protective covering on a seed, enclosing the embryo and its food supply. (A 61) When the leaves on a young plant start to grow and open up, the *seed coat* falls off.

seed dispersal The scattering of seeds away from the parent plant. (A88) The wind is one way in which *seed dispersal* is carried out.

seed leaf A first leaf found inside a seed, providing food for the tiny developing plant. (A66) A monocot seed contains one *seed leaf*.

seedling (sēd'liŋ) A young growing plant after it first sprouts and develops new leaves. (A66) In spring the forest floor is covered with green *seedlings*.

seed plant A plant that reproduces by forming seeds. (A78) Corn and wheat are *seed plants*.

semicircular canal Any of three curved tubelike structures of the inner ear that help the body to maintain balance. (F85) The *semicircular canals* respond to movements of the head.

sensory neuron (sen'sər ē nōō'rän) A nerve cell that carries impulses from the senses to the brain and spinal cord. (G28) *Sensory neurons* carry impulses from your eyes to your brain.

sexual reproduction The production of offspring that occurs when a male sex cell joins a female sex cell. (A59) The *sexual reproduction* of flowers is greatly aided by insects.

shoreline The ecosystem where land and ocean meet. (D54) The *shoreline* varies in width around the world.

simple microscope A microscope that uses a single lens to magnify objects. (F41) A magnifying glass is a *simple microscope*.

skeletal muscle Voluntary muscle tissue; also, one of the muscles that moves bones. (G17) Tendons attach *skeletal muscles* to bones.

skeletal system The system of bones and tissues that supports and protects the body. (G8) The human *skeletal system* contains 206 bones.

smelting (smelt'iŋ) The process of melting ore to remove the metal from it. (E28) Workers obtain iron by *smelting* iron ore in a blast furnace.

smooth muscle Involuntary muscle tissue that lines the inside of blood vessels, intestines, and other organs. (G17) *Smooth muscles* move food through the digestive system.

solar system The Sun and the planets and other objects that orbit the Sun. Also, any star and the objects that revolve around it. (B34) Our *solar system* consists of the Sun, nine known planets, and many smaller objects.

sound A form of energy that travels through matter as waves. (F56) The *sound* made the floor vibrate.

sound synthesizer (sound sin'thə sī zər) An electronic device that can produce a wide variety of sounds. (F71) The composer used a *sound synthesizer* to create a new musical composition.

sprain An injury in which the ligament at a joint is torn or twisted. (G19) An ankle *sprain* can take weeks to heal.

stamen (stā'mən) The male reproductive structure of a flower. (A16) Pollen is produced in the *stamens*.

star A huge object in space, made up of hot gases, that shines by its own light. (B17) Many *stars* are believed to have systems of planets.

starch (stärch) A substance found in plants that is a storage form of glucose. (A35) Potatoes contain a lot of *starch*.

stem The part of a plant that supports the leaves and flowers and carries water to these parts of the plant. (A12) The trunk of a tree is a *stem*.

steroid (stir'oid) A drug that helps to build up muscle tissue and strength. (G55) Some athletes have used *steroids*.

stimulant (stim'yoo lənt) A drug that increases the activity of the nervous system. (G55) Many people drink coffee because it acts as a *stimulant*.

stimulus (stim'yoo ləs) An event or environmental condition that triggers a nerve impulse, thus causing an organism to respond. (G28) The *stimulus* of a loud sound can make a person jump.

stoma (stō'mə; *pl.* stō ma'tə) One of many small openings, or pores, usually on the underside of a leaf, through which gases enter and leave a plant. (A46) The *stomata* on a water lily are on the top of the leaf.

strain An injury in which a muscle or tendon is torn slightly or stretched too far. (G20) Lifting the heavy couch gave me a back *strain*.

streak (strēk) The colored powder made by rubbing a mineral against a ceramic surface. (E15) Although pyrite is yellow, it produces a black *streak*.

substance abuse (sub'stəns ə-byoos') The improper use, or abuse, of alcohol or drugs. (G50) *Substance abuse* can damage a person's health.

supernova (soo'pər nō və) An exploding star. (B66) When a red giant star uses up all its fuel, it collapses and explodes in a *supernova*.

syncline (sin'klīn) A downward fold of rock layers. (E84) Forces in Earth pushing on rock formed a *syncline*.

taiga (tī′gə) A biome that contains many coniferous trees and in which rainfall is moderate. (D51) The *taiga* is south of the tundra.

taste bud A receptor on the surface of the tongue that responds to different substances and makes it possible to taste. (G38) There are only four basic types of *taste buds*.

tendon (ten′dən) A strong cord of tissue that joins a muscle to a bone. (G17) *Tendons* pull on bones like strings pull on the limbs of a puppet.

terrestrial planet (tə res′trē əl plan′it) An object in space that resembles Earth in size, in density, and in its mainly rocky composition. (B44) Mars is a *terrestrial planet*.

timbre (tam′bər) The quality of sound that sets one voice or musical instrument apart from another. (F58) The same note played on a violin and on a trumpet differ in *timbre*.

translucent (trans loo′sənt) Letting light through but scattering it; objects cannot be clearly seen through translucent material. (F48) The *translucent* glass dimmed the room.

transparent (trans per′ənt) Letting light through; objects can be clearly seen through transparent material. (F47) Window glass is usually *transparent* so that people can see through it.

transpiration (tran spə rā′shən) A process in which a plant releases moisture through its stomata. (A46) *Transpiration* adds water to the air.

tropical rain forest A biome distinguished by lush vegetation, abundant rainfall, and plentiful sunlight. (D50) The *tropical rain forest* supports the greatest variety of life of any biome.

tropism (trō′piz əm) A growth response of a plant to conditions in the environment, such as light or water. (A50) Growing toward a light source is an example of a plant *tropism*.

trough (trôf) The long narrow hollow between two waves. (F57) A *trough* occurs between two wave crests.

tundra (tun′drə) A biome characterized by cold temperatures and low precipitation. (D51) The *tundra* blooms in summer.

universe (yoon′ə vʉrs) The sum of everything that exists. (B70) Our solar system is part of the *universe*.

vacuole (vak′yoo ōl) A cell part that stores water and nutrients. (A24) Some plant cells have large *vacuoles*.

vacuum (vak'yōō əm) A space that is empty of any matter. (F17) Light waves can travel through a *vacuum.*

vibration A back-and-forth movement of matter. (F56) It is the *vibration* of the guitar strings that produces sound.

visible light A form of electromagnetic energy that can be seen. (F8) The eye responds to *visible light.*

volume The loudness or softness of a sound. (F78) Please turn up the *volume* on the radio.

water cycle A continuous process in which water moves between the atmosphere and Earth's surface, including its use by living things. (B87, D36) The *water cycle* is powered by energy from the Sun.

wave A disturbance that carries energy and that travels away from its starting point. (F17) The experiment measured how quickly light *waves* travel.

wavelength The distance between one crest of a wave and the next crest. (F17, F57) Red light has a longer *wavelength* than does blue light.

weathering The breaking up of rocks into sediments by such forces as wind, rain, and sunlight. (E62) Through *weathering*, igneous rock can be broken down into sediments.

wetland Any one of three ecosystems—marsh, swamp, or bog—where land and fresh water meet. (D53) *Wetlands* help purify water.

wheel and axle A simple machine made of two wheels of different sizes that pivot around the same point. (C58) A doorknob, along with its shaft, is an example of a *wheel and axle.*

white dwarf A very small, dying star that gives off very little light. (B65) When the Sun's fuel runs out, it will collapse into a *white dwarf.*

work The movement of a force through a distance. (C28) *Work* is done in lifting an object.

xylem cell (zī'ləm sel) A plant cell that, when joined with other similar cells, forms a transport system throughout a plant. (A11) The wood of a tree is formed mainly of *xylem cells.*

INDEX

* Activity

* Activity

CREDITS

Cover: *Design, Art Direction, and Production:* Design Five, NYC; *Photography:* Jade Albert; *Photography Production:* Picture It Corporation; *Illustration:* Deborah Haley Melmon. **TOC:** Dom Doyle, Patrick Gnan, Robert Pasternack, Michael Sloan, Elsa Warnick.

ILLUSTRATORS

UNIT 5A Chapter A1: Steve Buchanan: 12, 13, 15; Susan Johnston Carlson: 25; Fran Milner 24, 27; Patrick O'Brien: 18, 19, 20, 21; Walter Stuart: 10, 11. **Chapter A2:** David Barber: 38; Barbara Cousins: 34; Brad Gaber: 47; Patrick Gnan: 50, 51, 52; Carlyn Iverson: 36, 39; Merri Nelson: 46; Mary Ellen Niatas: 44, 45; Debra Page-Trim: 37. **Chapter A3:** Glory Bechtold: 59, 60, 61; Catherine Deeter: 66, 67; Eldon Doty: 68, 69; Wendy Smith-Griswold: 73. **Chapter A4:** Jennifer Hewitson: 82, 83; Karen Minot: 90, 91; Merri Nelson: 88, 89; Wendy Smith-Griswold: 78, 82, 83, 95; Elsa Warnick: 92, 93.

UNIT 5B Chapter B1: Delores Bego: 9; Michael Carroll: 14; Dale Glasgow & Assoc.: 10, 11; Jeff Hitch: 13; Fred Holz: 22; Tony Novak: 15; Tom Powers: 11, 27; Robert Schuster: 17; Jim Starr: 24, 25; Lane Yerkes: 21. **Chapter B2:** Michael Carroll: 38, 39, 50; Dennis Davidson: 34, 35, 42, 43; Dale Glasgow & Assoc.: 30, 36, 37, 40, 50; Joe LeMonnier: 72; Susan Melrath: 36, 37; Verlin Miller: 36; John O'Connor: 41; Robert Schuster: 44, 45, 47, 48, 49, 50. **Chapter B3:** Michael Carroll: 70; Joe LeMonnier: 72; Lu Matthews: 60, 61; Tom Powers: 57, 67, 71, 73; Joe Spencer: 64, 65. **Chapter B4:** Terry Boles: 79; Richard Courtney: 87; Dale Glasgow & Assoc.: 94; Nina Laden: 84; Andy Myer: 93; Scott Ross: 83; Stephen Wagner: 80, 86, 95.

UNIT 5C Chapter C1: Delores Bego: 35; Kieran Bergin: 18, 19; Ka Botzis: 22; Carolyn Bracken: 12; Sarah Jane English: 22, 23; Ron Fleming: 12; David Uhl: 20, 21; Arden Von Haeger: 32, 33; Richard Waldrep: 28, 29. **Chapter C2:** Andrea Baruffi: 43; Gregg Fitzhugh: 48, 49, 53, 54, 55, 63; Dale Glasgow & Assoc.: 50, 51; Patrick Gnan: 58, 59; Susan Hunt Yule: 44, 45; A. J. Miller: 60; Miles Parnell: 43, 44, 45; Michael Sloan: 61, 62; Leslie Wolf: 53, 54.

UNIT 5D Chapter D1: Lori Anzalone: 20; Patrick Gnan: 8, 9; Robert Hynes Studio: 10, 11; Jim Salvati: 12, 13; Wendy Smith-Griswold: 17. **Chapter D2:** David Barber: 28; Andy Lendway: 30, 31, 43; Jim Starr: 38; Don Stewart: 34, 35, 36, 37, 41, 42. **Chapter D3:** Joe LeMonnier: 56; Paul Mirocha: 52, 53, 54, 55; Carlos Ochagauia: 59; Rodica Prato: 48, 49, 50, 51.

UNIT 5E Chapter E1: Jeanette Adams: 28; Lingta Kung: 12, 13, 14, 15, 16; Bill Morse: 30, 31; Wendy Smith-Griswold: 20, 21. **Chapter E2:** Terry Boles: 61, 63; Brad Gaber: 40, 58, 59; Robert Pasternack: 47; Scot Ritchie: 54; Robert Schuster: 49; Michael Sloan: 60. **Chapter E3:** Absolute Science: 71, 77; Eldon Doty: 76; Dale Glasgow & Assoc.: 68, 69, 95; J.A.K. Graphics: 78; Joe LeMonnier: 85, 93; Susan Melrath: 78, 79; Verlin Miller: 86; Robert Pasternack: 85, 91; Tom Powers: 67; Scot Ritchie: 70; Jim Starr: 87.

UNIT 5F Chapter F1: Jeanette Adams: 16; Bob Brugger: 25, 27; Michael Carroll: 8, 9; Jim Deigan: 22; Eldon Doty: 12; Susan Hunt Yule: 26; Robert Pasternack: 17, 18, 19; Scot Ritchie: 8. **Chapter F2:** Rose Berlin: 51; Bob Bredemeier: 39; Marie Dauenheimer: 33, 35; Jim Fanning: 45; J.A.K. Graphics: 32, 34; George Kelvin: 36, 37; Andy Miller: 43; Len Morgan: 47. **Chapter F3:** Mark Bender: 69; Terry Boles: 62, 63; Roger Chandler: 68, 69; Dale Glasgow & Assoc.: 56, 57, 59; Tom Lochray: 66, 67; Larry Moore: 71, 72; Terry Ravanelli: 72. **Chapter F4:** Tim Blough: 94; Marty Bucella: 78; Dale Glasgow & Assoc.: 93, 94; Dale Gustafson: 91, 92; Ellen Going Jacobs: 85; Ray Vella: 78, 79, 95.

UNIT 5G Chapter G1: May Cheney: 8, 9, 10, 11; Kathleen Dunne: 8, 19, 20, 21, 22; Jackie Heda: 12, 19, 20; Bob Swanson: 13; Kate Sweeney: 17, 18, 23. **Chapter G2:** Scott Barrows: 30, 31; Eldon Doty: 40, 41; Dom Doyle: 28; Marcia Hartsock: 37, 38, 39, 42, 45; Jackie Heda: 31; Jane Hurd: 31, 32; Robert Margulies: 33; Steve McInturff: 44; Briar Lee Mitchell: 29. **Chapter G3:** Medical Art Co.: 59, 63; Bob Novak: 50, 51, 53; Ray Vella: 52, 61.

Glossary: Lori Anzalone, Patrick Gnan, Carlyn Iverson, Fran Milner, Robert Pasternack.

Handbook: Kathleen Dunne, Laurie Hamilton, Catherine Leary, Andy Meyer

PHOTOGRAPHS

All photographs by Silver Burdett Ginn (SBG) unless otherwise noted.

Unit A Opener 1: *border* G. Shih-R. Kessel/Visuals Unlimited. **Chapter 1** 4–5: *bkgd.* Will Houghton/Fairchild Tropical Garden, Miami; *insets* Courtesy, Fairchild Tropical Gardens. 6–9: Ken Karp for SBG. 10: Alfred Pasieka/Peter Arnold. 12: © John Buitenkant/Photo Researchers, Inc. 13: © Cecil Fox/Science Source/Photo Researchers, Inc. 14: *t.* © Jerome Wexler/Photo Researchers, Inc.; *b.* Milton Rand/Tom Stack & Associates. 15: *l.* Milton Rand/Tom Stack & Associates; *r.* © Scott Camamzine/Photo Researchers, Inc. 16: *l.* E. R. Degginger/Color-Pic, Inc.; *r.* © Arthur Beck/Photo Researchers, Inc. 17: *t.* © Anthony Mercieca/Photo Researchers, Inc.; *b.l.* Brokaw Photography/Visuals Unlimited; *b.m.* Rod Planck/Tom Stack & Associates; *b.r.* John Gerlach/Visuals Unlimited. 19: *t.* © Blair Seitz/Photo Researchers, Inc.; *b.* Gary Milburn/Tom Stack & Associates; *inset*

Ken Karp for SBG. 20: Ken Karp for SBG. 21: *l.* David Cavagnaro/Peter Arnold; *r.* E. R. Degginger/Color-Pic, Inc. 22–23: Ken Karp for SBG. 26: *t.* © Angelina Lax/Photo Researchers, Inc.; *m.* © Bill Bachman/Photo Researchers, Inc.; *b.* Greg Vaughn/Tom Stack & Associates. **Chapter 2** 28–29: *bkgd.* © Jack Dermid/Photo Researchers, Inc.; *inset* Richard Hutchings for SBG. 30–32: Ken Karp for SBG. 33: *bkgd.* Phil Degginger/Color-Pic, Inc.; *inset* Tom Stack/Tom Stack & Associates. 34: © Science Source/Photo Researchers, Inc. 35: *m.b.* Ken Karp for SBG. 37: *t.* © Ray Ellis/Photo Researchers, Inc.; *m.t.,m.b.,* *b.* E. R. Degginger/Color-Pic, Inc.; 40–43: Ken Karp for SBG. 46: *bkgd.* Phil Degginger/Color-Pic, Inc.; *inset* © Andrew Syred/Science Photo Library/Photo Researchers, Inc. 47: © Dr. Jeremy Burgess/Science Photo Library/Photo Researchers, Inc. 48–49: Ken Karp for SBG. 50: Runk/Schoenberger/Grant Heilman Photography. 52: *t.l.* © Franz Krenn/Photo Researchers, Inc.; *t.r.* Jim Strawser/Grant Heilman Photography; *b.l.* Amanda Merullo/Stock Boston; *b.r.* Foster/Bruce Coleman. **Chapter 3** 54–55: Royal Botanic Gardens, Sydney. 56–58: Grant Huntington for SBG. 60: *t.* © E. R. Degginger/Photo Researchers, Inc.; *b.* © Dr. Jeremy Burgess/Science Photo Library/Photo Researchers, Inc. 61: Dwight R. Kuhn. 62: *t.l., t.r.* Greg Vaughn/Tom Stack & Associates; *b.l.* © Phillipe Plailly/Science Photo Library/Photo Researchers, Inc.; *b.r.* © Takeshi Takahara/Photo Researchers, Inc. 63: *t.* Greg Vaughn/Tom Stack & Associates; *b.* Peter Ziminski/Visuals Unlimited. 67: Runk/Schoenberger/Grant Heilman Photography. 69: Bruce Coleman. 70: *l.* S. J. Krasemann/Peter Arnold; *r.* Sharon Gerig/Tom Stack & Associates. 71: © Jack Dermid/Photo Researchers. 72: *l.* David Sieren/Visuals Unlimited; *r.* Grant Heilman Photography. **Chapter 4** 74–75: *bkgd.* Zoological Society of San Diego; *L. inset* Ron Garrison/Zoological Society of San Diego; *R. inset* Ken Kelley. 76: *l.* © Rod Planck/Photo Researchers, Inc.; *r.* Phil Degginger/Color-Pic, Inc. 77: Ken Karp for SBG. 79: *t.l.* Runk/Schoenberger/Grant Heilman Photography; *t.r.* © Alvin E. Staffan/Photo Researchers, Inc.; *b.* K. G. Preston Mafham/Earth Scenes. 80: Runk/Schoenberger/Grant Heilman Photography. 80–81: Richard Kolar/Earth Scenes. 81: *t.* Richard Shiell/Earth Scenes; *b.l.* Alan Pitcairn/Grant Heilman Photography; *b.r.* Carl Wolinsky/Stock Boston. 84: Ken Karp for SBG. 86: *l.* Runk/Schoenberger/Grant Heilman Photography; *r.* David M. Dennis/Tom Stack & Associates. 87: *t.* C. C. Lockwood/DRK Photo; *b.* Lee Rentz/Bruce Coleman. 88: *l.* Raymond A. Mendez/Animals Animals; *r.* Breck P. Kent. 89: *t.l.* S. Nielsen/DRK Photo; *t.r.* Arthur C. Smith III/Grant Heilman Photography; *m.l.* Inga Spence/Tom Stack & Associates; *m.r.* © Richard Parker/Photo Researchers, Inc.; *b.* Laura Riley/Bruce Coleman. 90–91: Arthur C. Smith III/Grant Heilman Photography. 91: *t.* C. C. Lockwood/Bruce Coleman; *b.* © 1996 Eastcot/Mornatiuk/Woodfin Camp & Associates. 94: Dr. Nigel Smith/Earth Scenes.

Unit B Opener 1: *border* Roger Ressmeyer/Starlight. **Chapter 1** 4: *inset* Roger Ressmeyer/Starlight. 5: *inset* Alan Levenson/Time Magazine. 6–8: Grant Huntington for SBG. 10: © John Sanford & David Parker/Science Photo Library/Photo Researchers, Inc. 12: Roger Ressmeyer/Starlight. 16: © Gordon Garradd/Science Photo Library/Photo Researchers, Inc. 18–20: Grant Huntington for SBG. 21: Dennis Di Cicco. 22: Roger Ressmeyer/Starlight. 23: The Stock Market. 24: Frank P. Rossotto/Stocktrek. 25: © European Space Agency/Science Photo Library/Photo Researchers, Inc. 26: *t.* Andrea Pistolesi/The Image Bank; *b.* Stocktrek Photo Agency. **Chapter 2** 28: *bkgd.* NASA/Photri. 29: *inset* Roger Ressmeyer/Starlight. 44: *bkgd.* Michael Campbell for SBG; *l.* JPL/NASA; *t.r.* NASA JPL/Starlight; *b.r.* NASA/Peter Arnold. 45: *bkgd.* Michael Campbell for SBG; *t.l.* NASA/Tom Stack & Associates; *m.l.* NASA/Photri; *b.l.* Sovfoto/Eastfoto; *t.r.* Stocktrek ; *b.r.* USGS, Flagstaff, Arizona/Starlight. 46: *bkgd.* Michael Campbell for SBG; *t.l.* JPL/NASA; *t.r* D. Simonelli/Cornell University; *b.* NASA/JPL/Phil Degginger. 47: *bkgd.* Michael Campbell for SBG; *l.* NASA/Tom Stack & Associates; *t.r.* USGS/TSADO/Tom Stack & Associates; *b.r.* Frank Rossotto/Tom Stack & Associates. 48: *bkgd.* Michael Campbell for SBG; *t.* NASA/The Image Bank; *m.* JPL/NASA; *b.l.* NASA/JPL/TSADO/Tom Stack & Associates; *b.r.* NASA/Bruce Coleman. 49: *bkgd.* Michael Campbell for SBG; *t.l., b.l., b.r.* JPL/NASA; *t.r.* © NASA/Science Source/Photo Researchers, Inc. 50: *bkgd.* Michael Campbell for SBG; *inset* NASA/Tom Stack & Associates. **Chapter 3** 52: *bkgd.* Harald Sund/The Image Bank. 53: *inset* Bob Sacha. 54–59: Ken Karp for SBG. 62: *l., r.* © Royal Observatory, Edinburgh/AATB/Science Photo Library/Photo Researchers, Inc.; *m.* Photri. 63: *l.* Anglo-Australian Telescope Board; *m.* National Optical Astronomy Observatories/Phil Degginger; *r.* © Royal Observatory, Edinburgh/Science Photo Library/Photo Researchers, Inc. 67: E. R. Degginger/Color-Pic, Inc. 68: *l.* NASA/Peter Arnold; *m.* Photri; *r.* © Royal Observatory, Edinburgh/Science Photo Library/Photo Researchers, Inc. 69: *l., r.* Anglo-Australian Telescope Board; *m.* Frank P. Rossotto; 70: Kazwaki Iwasaki/The Stock Market. **Chapter 4** 74–75: *bkgd.* NASA/Silver Burdett Ginn; *inset* Richard T. Nowitz. 81: NASA. 85: Bruce Coleman. 89: Donna McLaughlin/The Stock Market. 90: The Arecibo Observatory/National Astronomy and Ionosphere Center/Cornell University. 91: Photri.

Unit C Opener 1: *border* © Tony Craddock/Science Photo Library/Photo Researchers, Inc. **Chapter 1** 4: *bkgd, r. inset* Dan Feicht; *inset* Courtesy, Arrow Dynamics, Inc. 6–8: Ken Karp for SBG. 9: © Holway & Lobel/Globus Studios for SBG. 10: *l.* Ben Rose/The Image Bank; *r.* Jean-Claude Leveune/Stock Boston. 11: Grant Huntington for SBG. 13: Richard Hutchings for SBG. 14–16: Ken Karp for SBG. 18: *m.* Duomo; *r.* International Stock Photos. 20: Robert Frerck/Odyssey Productions. 23: Ed Hille/The Stock Market. 24–27: Ken Karp for SBG. 31: *t.* Richard Hutchings for SBG; *b.* Richard Hutchings/PhotoEdit. 34: Bob Winsett/Tom Stack & Associates. **Chapter 2** 36–37: *bkgd.* Martin A. Levick; *inset* Focus on Sports. 38–41: Ken Karp for SBG. 42: Ellis Herwig/Stock Boston. 43: *l.* Erich Lessing/Art Resource; *r.* B. Wilson/Sheridan Photo Library. 46–49: Ken Karp for SBG. 50: Grant Huntington for SBG. 51: *t.* Ken Karp for SBG; *b.* © Jerry Wachter/Photo Researchers, Inc. 52: *l.* Grant Huntington for SBG; *m.* Tony Freeman/PhotoEdit; *r.* Bob Daemmrich/Stock Boston. 56–57: Ken Karp for SBG. 58: Richard Hutchings for SBG. 60: The Bettman Archive.

Unit D Opener 1: *border* Ben Edwards/Tony Stone Images. **Chapter 1** 4–5: *bkgd.* Manfred Kage/Peter Arnold; *l. inset* Mark Smith; *r. inset* Courtesy, Site Redemption Services. 12: *t.* © David Weintraub/Photo Researchers, Inc.; *b.r.* © Farrell Grehan/Photo Researchers, Inc.; *b.l.* Jon Feingersh/Stock Boston. 13: *l.* John Stern/Earth Scenes; *m.t., m.b., t.r.* Gary Braasch; *b.r.* © Pat and Tom Leeson/Photo Researchers, Inc. 15: David Phillips for SBG. 16: © John Bova/Photo Researchers, Inc. 18: *t.* Alan G. Nelson/Animals Animals; *b.* Adrienne T. Gibson/Animals Animals. 19: *t.* Laura Riley/Bruce Coleman; *b.* P. Welmann/Animals Animals. 20: Carl R. Sams II/Peter Arnold. 22: *l.* © Tom Evans/Photo Researchers, Inc.; *m.* © Lew Eatherton/Photo Researchers, Inc.; *r.* E. R. Degginger/Earth Scenes. 23: © Stephen Dalton/Photo Researchers, Inc. **Chapter 2** 24–25: *bkgd.* S. Nielsen/Imagery.